# REPOSSIBLE BOX SET 1 (BOOKS 3-5)

ASK, DARE, CREATE

BRADLEY CHARBONNEAU

# CONTENTS

*Introduction*   vii

## ASK

| | |
|---|---|
| Preface | 5 |
| Prologue | 11 |
| Foreword | 15 |

PART I
### ALLOW

| | |
|---|---|
| 1. Answer | 21 |
| 2. Attitude | 23 |
| 3. Awkward | 24 |
| 4. Anything | 28 |

PART II
### SERVE

| | |
|---|---|
| 5. Solve | 33 |
| 6. Silence | 35 |
| 7. Steek | 38 |
| 8. Say No | 41 |
| 9. Sucker | 44 |

PART III
### KNOW

| | |
|---|---|
| 10. Knowledge | 51 |
| 11. Kids | 55 |
| 12. Killer | 59 |
| 13. Keep | 61 |

| | |
|---|---|
| Afterword | 63 |
| Acknowledgments | 65 |
| About the Author | 67 |
| The End | 68 |

# DARE

| | |
|---|---:|
| Preface | 71 |
| Preface | 77 |
| Introduction | 79 |
| Prologue | 83 |
| Foreword | 85 |

### PART I
## DO

| | |
|---|---:|
| 1. Do | 89 |
| 2. Dream | 91 |
| 3. Deadline | 95 |
| 4. Don't | 99 |

### PART II
## ADJUST

| | |
|---|---:|
| 5. Adjust | 103 |
| 6. Ask | 105 |
| 7. Aim | 108 |
| 8. Ally | 113 |

### PART III
## RECEIVE

| | |
|---|---:|
| 9. Receive | 121 |
| 10. Refresh | 123 |
| 11. Rehearse | 126 |
| 12. Roar | 129 |

### PART IV
## ELEVATE

| | |
|---|---:|
| 13. Elevate | 135 |
| 14. Empty | 138 |
| 15. Educate | 141 |
| 16. Escape | 144 |
| Afterword | 149 |
| Acknowledgments | 151 |
| About the Author | 153 |
| The End | 155 |

# CREATE

| | |
|---|---|
| Preface | 163 |
| Introduction | 167 |
| Foreword | 171 |
| "Boost Your Brand with a Book" | 173 |

### PART I
## WELCOME

| | |
|---|---|
| 1. Are you waiting for someone to ask you? | 179 |
| 2. Bouquets of flowers, men in suits, somber faces | 181 |
| 3. Here to Create | 186 |
| 4. Live, Work, Create. Pick one. | 188 |

### PART II
## CHALLENGE

| | |
|---|---|
| 5. How will you define success? | 193 |
| 6. What if you don't know what your passion is? | 195 |
| 7. Via Negativa | 197 |
| 8. When is the absolute perfect time to start your masterpiece? | 200 |

### PART III
## REPEAT

| | |
|---|---|
| 9. The Habit is the Goal | 205 |
| 10. Offense & Defense | 207 |
| 11. 5-Word Hooks and Constraint Breeds Creativity | 209 |
| 12. Trigger Daily Clarity | 213 |

### PART IV
## EDUCATE

| | |
|---|---|
| 13. What if your input is Netflix and Instagram? | 219 |
| 14. Give the Gift of You | 221 |
| 15. How you make them feel | 223 |
| 16. Just Stop (for the Day) | 226 |
| 17. Creating creates more creativity ... even while driving a car | 228 |

### PART V
## AMPLIFY

| | |
|---|---|
| 18. Lacking creativity? Tune into your radio frequency. | 233 |

| | |
|---|---|
| 19. Creating is Fun! | 237 |
| 20. "I have nothing to offer." | 239 |
| 21. You are not alone | 241 |
| 22. Feeling stuck? Bogged down? Pop that boil, let it out, create. | 243 |
| 23. Are you working on another book? | 247 |

PART VI
## TRUST

| | |
|---|---|
| 24. Oh no, not the apocalypse! | 251 |
| 25. There are no gazelles in therapy | 254 |
| 26. From "Why me?" to "Why not me?" | 255 |
| 27. Shoot off the flare gun of your passion and see who takes notice | 257 |
| 28. Cre8 | 259 |
| 29. A 14-year-old teenager, a 20-minute drive. Do we have time to create? | 263 |

PART VII
## EVOLVE

| | |
|---|---|
| 30. Do something daring, find tribe, write book. | 267 |
| 31. "I measure my life by what I create." | 270 |
| 32. Afraid it isn't real | 273 |
| 33. Tony | 275 |
| 34. How to go from Nothing to Everything | 277 |
| 35. Meditate + Create | 280 |

PART VIII
## THANK YOU

| | |
|---|---|
| 36. A dialogue without an audience is a monologue | 285 |
| 37. Thank you, mom | 287 |
| Ask | 289 |
| About the Author | 291 |
| Acknowledgments | 295 |
| Also by Bradley Charbonneau | 299 |
| The End | 302 |

| | |
|---|---|
| *Afterword* | 303 |

# INTRODUCTION

Welcome to the first Repossible box set!

If you've arrived here new to the series, here is the entire lineup:

1. Repossible
2. Every Single Day
3. **Ask**
4. **Dare**
5. **Create**
6. Decide
7. Meditate
8. Spark
9. Surrender
10. Play
11. Celebrate
12. Evaluate
13. Elevate

The first book, Repossible, is an introduction to the series and the rest of the books.

Every Single Day is both an introduction to the case study of the first Repossible experiment as well as something of an autobiography.

I come back to the dentist again and again:

"Which teeth do you want to keep?"

— THE DENTIST

It's the same with "Which life do we want to live?" but also, "How many days per year do you want to be the person you've dreamed of being?"

Our personalities are not like the carved in stone caricatures on Mount Rushmore. They are malleable and we can change them if—and only if—we truly, deeply want to.

So the question remains and it's a first one to enter into the book called Ask:

Who will you be next?

Bradley Charbonneau

REPOSSIBLE BOOK 3

# ASK

WHAT IF THE ANSWER IS YES?

**BRADLEY CHARBONNEAU**

"Everything you want is out there waiting for you to ask. Everything you want also wants you. But you have to take action to get it."

— Jules Renard

# PREFACE

I know. This book hasn't even started. But I'm going to dare do the impossible: *ask* you a question.

See how easy that was? I didn't even write a page yet and I'm walking the talk, I'm doing the deed, I'm daring to ask.

- Allow
- Serve
- Know

What you have in your hands is a book. Or maybe you have the audiobook and then it's in your ears.

Although I'm an author at heart, I see a *trajectory of connection* that goes something like this:

1. **Read** (those things you read in a book or article)
2. **Hear** (what we hear, voices, music, podcasts, audiobooks)
3. **See** (we use our eyes to experience, we can see gestures, facial expressions, etc.)
4. **Feel** (this can come from any of this list but it's usually not physical, it's how it makes your gut react)

5. **Touch** (although this sounds like we're shaking hands or giving a hug—and that's part of it—it's more physiological than necessarily physical)
6. **Resonate** (this one is in your heart, when this happens, it tingles the hairs on your arms and possibly releases a flock of butterflies in your belly)

If you have the book or ebook or audiobook in your hands, see how far—or rather, not far—we are down this path?

I want to take it further.

This is possibly your first taste of Repossible and I want to invite you to more. Come on over to ask.repossible.com and sign up, for free, to go deeper down this trajectory of communication.

We'll have audio, video, downloads, and a community of Repossible-istas to connect with, dare I say *resonate* with, and unlock the cage of butterflies and get those hairs standing on end on your arms and neck.

Repossible is a series of books, podcasts, and video. We are mini-courses online, Saturday afternoon workshops. We are people. We are creators. We're a 3-day "Retreat to the Repossible" long weekend. We are, together, a week in Bali for a "Repossible Your Life" getaway and life-altering experience. Several days in a place you've never been—I've never been. Yet.

I know, I could have just said:

*"Come join us at ask.repossible.com for free bonus content!"*

but as you'll see, I tend to not follow too many rules and do things in a way that I think, although it might not make sense early on (OK, fine, it may never make sense…), it will sink in.

I'm in this for **The Long Game.** I'm all for easy wins and quick victories but we're not talking about "one of the nine lives we have as a cat." I don't know about you but I have just one life and this is it.

See, I haven't even started and I'm already WAY out of my (former) comfort zone as I just asked you directly to come connect with us.

That wasn't so bad, was it?

But now you have a choice:

1. Turn the page and continue reading
2. Type in ask.repossible.com and sign in

You can choose the order but I challenge you to do #2 first.

# DEDICATION

*To those who **ask** the kids the three most delightful words of power we can transfer from one human to another:*

**"Then what happened?"**

*It's with those three words that I, together with my two boys, wrote one of my first books.*
*All I had to do was Ask.*

# PROLOGUE

> "The fact that you are willing to say, 'I do not understand, and it is fine,' is the greatest understanding you could exhibit."
>
> — Wayne Dyer

Since I've graduated from the *School of Not Asking* and am now in the part-time accreditation program of *Asking All the Time*, I need to revisit my days of fear.

It's a Friday afternoon as I write this. I just got a text from my 16-year-old son Liam that he didn't do very well on his German test.

His mother and I speak fluent German. I asked him yesterday (and over the past two years…) if I could help him with studying.

- I asked.
- I begged.
- I pleaded.

Then I forced it and just spoke German and kept at it.

But he wasn't having any of it. He wanted to do it his way. He didn't want our help. He said he was *fine*. He had a *good study session*.

Had he received a good grade, this would have all been fine. Had he any sort of grasp on German, I'd be OK with this.

But he didn't and he doesn't.

- He didn't ask for help.
- He even refused help.
- He's 16.
- He's a boy.

I sent him a text after his test saying something along the lines of how asking for help was not a sign of weakness but rather **those who are strong ask questions to become even stronger.**

Yes, not only do I put brilliant quotes in the beginnings of chapters of my books, I also send texts to my kids.

You are voluntarily reading this book. Well, unless you're in a prison in Thailand and this was the only English book left on the cart.

But for my kids, I like to think that they "hear me even if they're not listening."

Maybe they want the answers even though they don't dare ask.

I have long gotten over my fear of asking. I ask for anything—and everything—these days. No shame. No fear. No problem.

Sure, I get in trouble. But what I really want to do is **begin the conversation.**

That's what I'm doing here with you.

You see, I have no idea where you are along the spectrum of Ask.

1. You don't dare
2. You might but you don't really want the answer—or want to talk about it
3. You don't really want to know at all
4. You ask a bit—but maybe just the easy stuff
5. You ask the medium stuff
6. You can deal the hard stuff
7. You want the hard stuff and relish it

8. You're practically a mercenary "ask" professional who even asks for those who don't dare

But I want to start from the beginning. It's almost a birth or a seed sprouting from its little egg or shell or…whatever it is that a seed comes from.

See? I'm asking questions already. "Where does a seed come from? What does it break out of?"

I don't know. I'm asking.

I'm not afraid to ask the silly stuff.

You know why?

Because it's practice. Then I get more used to it and I can ask the harder stuff:

1. What is this next paragraph about?
2. What is this book about?
3. What is the Repossible series really uncovering?
4. Who am I to write it?

Wow. Dang.

Pipe down there, Pendergrass.

See how quickly things can get out of hand?

Let's stick to the easy stuff at first. For example:

*"Should we turn the page and get started with asking?"*

# FOREWORD
## BY MAI PHUTUR SELPH

"What if the answer is yes?"

— Mai Phutur Selph (asking the present-day Bradley Charbonneau)

My name is Mai. It sounds like My. Last name: Selph. Grandparents were Scottish. Maybe a little skittish. Middle name: Phutur. I think there are some Vietnamese ancestors along the way somewhere.

I wanted to write this forward and address it to a certain Mr. Bradley Charbonneau back before he became an author.

I could keep this really short and just ask him the question I asked him all of those years back but I should give you a little back story first.

Now, I know he's unique and no one has ever had thoughts like this but here's what he was worried about:

"What if who I want to become, what if I can actually accomplish it? What if it's not just possible in the theoretical sense but what if it's possible for me? Can I honest and truly become an author, a speaker, a teacher and will it happen in this lifetime?"

— Dear dear poor Mr. Charbonneau, years back

Ach. Poor boy.

There are really two questions. Some of know the answer to the first one but it's, oddly, the second question that often trips us up, stops us in our tracks, and puts on the slow road to nowhere.

1. Who will you be next?
2. What if the answer is yes?

Many people struggle with that first one. They don't really know or they don't want to admit it or it doesn't fit into "what I think I'm supposed to answer" or they just don't bother answering because they don't think it could ever possibly happen.

Mr. Charbonneau knew he wanted to be next (author, speaker, teacher). He was having a bit more trouble with that second question.

1. What if it were possible?
2. What if it were possible for me?

He knew there were writers and speakers and teachers in the world but he couldn't quite get past the idea that he could do it, that for him, the answer could be in the affirmative, that the answer really didn't come because he didn't ask the question, but when asking about your future and even having an inkling as to what you'd like for that next phase of your life, the weirdly scary answer is: yes.

1. Yes, it's possible.
2. Yes, it's possible for me.

He doesn't talk about it much but Mr. Charbonneau spent years, YEARS, knowing that it was possible for other people but he got stuck when it came to him.

The fear of success was actually greater than the fear of failure.

Failure was easy: try again, make excuses, wait a while. We all know failure. It's bizarrely easier to process.

But success? When the answer is yes?

Now what?!

Wait, now we have to go then do that thing, be that person, become that next phase of life that we have been dreaming about.

Let's do a little exercise.

Say my name out loud:

*Mai Phutur Selph*

Now let me ask you the same question I asked Mr. Charbonneau. However, if I could offer a little advice? Just a smidgen of consulting?

Don't wait so long to take action.

Don't wait until a family member dies so you then feel like it's now OK to do what you know you've wanting to do.

Don't take decades to answer, take seconds.

Don't dilly. Don't dally.

You know what it is you want to do. You know who it is you want to become.

Could you say my name again aloud?

*Mai Phutur Selph*

Take a deep breath. Close your eyes.

OK, wait, it's going to be hard to read the next line with your eyes closed. Unless you're listening to this on audiobook.

Hold off on closing your eyes just for a second.

Here's what I'd like to ask you. Remember, this is Mai Phutur Selph and I'm asking you right here, right now, in the foreword of this book.

Are you ready?

If you're reading, look at the words on the next line. Now let me ask you just this one question.

*What if the answer is yes?*

Mai Phutur Selph

Right Here

Right Now

# PART I

# ALLOW

"A person who never made a mistake never tried anything new."

— Albert Einstein

# 1

# ANSWER

THE ANSWER SLUMBERS IN THE QUESTION

"We get wise by asking questions, and even if these are not answered, we get wise, for a well-packed question carries its answer on its back as a snail carries its shell."

— James Stephens

*J*ust in case you missed the quote above, here is part of it again:

"... a well-packed question carries its answer on its back as a snail carries its shell."

This book is called Ask and, very consciously, not called answer.

I just want to flip upside down any preconceived ideas we might be coming into this book with.

We're looking to ask the questions, ask for help, ask how we can help.

Not so much give answers.

Sure, answers are lightning.

But asking is thunder.

- **Possible:** Answer
- **Impossible:** Avoid
- **Repossible:** Ask

## 2

# ATTITUDE
I HAVE A QUESTION

"You cannot control what happens to you, but you can control your attitude toward what happens to you, and in that, you will be mastering change rather than allowing it to master you."

— Brian Tracy

We're very early on in both this book as well as the entire Repossible series.

You may be new to my work but here goes a taste: I tend to look at things from a slightly different perspective.

Although we might learn "how to ask questions" in this book, what I'm really after is an "**Attitude of Asking.**"

Asking is more of a *mindset* than an *action*.

We'll get into nasty emotions like *fear* and scary concepts like *failure* but if we can adopt an Attitude of Asking, it's going to make this whole thing that much easier.

- **Possible:** Ask
- **Impossible:** Failure
- **Repossible:** The Asking Mindset

---
3
---

# AWKWARD
THAT SILENCE WHEN YOU DON'T KNOW WHAT TO ANSWER

> "Do the thing you fear most and the death of fear is certain."
>
> — Mark Twain

*I*'m just going to blow this whole fear open and come right and ask:

**Who will you be next?**

I was always waiting to be asked.

- To the party
- To help with the project
- To launch the book
- To be on the team
- To play the game
- What I'm working on
- What I had planned
- Who I would be next

If you're waiting for someone to ask you, here's me asking.
https://bradleycharbonneau.com/asking/

My work, my books, my pretty-much-everything has gotten better since I've opened up to, you know, those other humans who live on the planet for their interpretation of things.

*They* meaning *you*.

Your stories, your experiences, your opinions.

What do you say?

Here's my challenge to you:

- 15 minutes
- On the phone
- No guarantees
- No requirements
- Just talking about the verb *ask*

Maybe we don't get anywhere, maybe we end up talking about perfecting the burrito outside of the southwestern US (which is not a bad thing...).

Maybe we find one tiny nugget in our 15 minutes of conversation that merits its own chapter.

Maybe it's an entire section.

Maybe it starts with the letter a... or s... or k...

I digress.

A short time ago, I wouldn't have *dared ask* you to talk on the phone with me for 15 minutes.

I was scared.

Of what, I'm not sure but those are the worst fears: the ones we don't really understand.

Dare to have a chat?

https://bradleycharbonneau.com/asking/

Or we could talk about one of these verbs below.

**Repossible**

1. Repossible
2. Every Single Day
3. Ask
4. Dare
5. Create
6. Decide
7. Meditate
8. Spark
9. Surrender
10. Play
11. Celebrate
12. Evaluate
13. Elevate

All under the larger idea of Repossible.

Just that one word. What does it mean for you?

I know, we're here in this "book" and I put it in quotes because maybe the typical sense of a book is a bunch of words strung together by an author.

This is where I strive to make this more. A conversation, a discussion, a question, maybe an answer.

But not just from me. Not just Bradley Charbonneau and his ideas and questions and answers.

If this were a video, I would look into the camera and talk directly to you.

If we were in a room or a hall, I would come to you and ask to shake your hand.

This book is more than words on a page. It's an invitation to come out and ask. You can start with me.

I'm friendly. I swear.

This chapter is titled Awkward.

Is it still awkward? Have I breached that divide?

OK, fine, it's a little awkward, I'll give you that.

But once we get over that, watch how much better things will be. That "awkward" phase is always short.

Like when you meet new people at a party. A few sentences, offer some spinach dip, and it's over.

Just like that.

So there you go.

Spinach dip?

- **Possible:** Awkward
- **Impossible:** Avoid
- **Repossible:** Awesome

P.S. This is a slightly insane thing to do in a book so if you're seeing this, lucky you, as I'll probably pull it at some point.

## 4

# ANYTHING
ASK ME ANYTHING

"I know you've heard it a thousand times before. But it's true - hard work pays off. If you want to be good, you have to practice, practice, practice. If you don't love something, then don't do it."

— Ray Bradbury

Not because I know everything, but I might know something you don't know.

I'm not quite hip enough to have known where this came from, but when you start searching Google for anything that has the word "ask" in it, you come across stuff you didn't know. That's research.

**I wasn't really sure what the "Ask Me Anything" event was all about.**

The Atlantic does an excellent job in summing up how the concept of Ask Me Anything started:

> In 1992, a book debuted called Ask Me Anything: A Sex Therapist Answers the Most Important Questions for the 90's.
> KnowYourMeme says there was a mid-'90s AOL chatroom called, "Ask Me Anything" in the romance category. (Though it had

disappeared by 1999, when the Internet Archive began capturing data on aol.com.)

— FROM THE EVENT MANAGER BLOG

Of course, if someone "uninteresting" opened up an Ask Me Anything session, it might not garner that kind of attention. But in this case, a sex therapist? I suppose we all want to know what she knows!

I see this fall into a "knowledge" question.

1. **I know** something, more than you, things you'd like to know.
2. You get to **ask** me.

I see the allure. Especially with celebrities or people who "know lots that we don't know."

## Breaking Down Barriers

What the "Ask Me Anything" is doing is breaking down a wall that's usually in between the two people. Usually, you can't ask a celebrity anything. Or a brain surgeon. Or, I don't know, an author.

It's an invitation to something that is usually:

- Out of our reach,
- Expensive,
- Not in our sphere of connections.

What if you hosted an "Ask Me Anything" session? What would they ask you? What might you not answer? What would be the hard questions you'd answer?

What if you could ask anyone you wanted anything? It's a bit of a test of your curiosity.

Because let's face it, if you're not curious, you're not going to ask the questions.

If you're not curious about something, if you don't have questions, it's probably a subject you don't care so much about.

Let's start with easy questions you'd like to ask famous people—or any people.

Just for fun, write down a few questions for famous people you would like to ask.

Remember, asking is a muscle and you can get better at it.

- **Possible:** Don't ask anyone anything
- **Impossible:** Ask the Warren commission who shot JFK
- **Repossible:** Write down your question—and ask it to someone less famous

# PART II

# SERVE

"Successful people are always looking for opportunities to help others. Unsuccessful people are always asking, 'What's in it for me?'"

— Brian Tracy

# 5

## SOLVE

LOOKING FOR ANSWERS? SOLVE SOMEONE ELSE'S QUESTION.

> "We cannot solve our problems with the same thinking we used when we created them."
>
> — ALBERT EINSTEIN

*A* friend of mine in the public speaking world gave a talk called "Cheer" where he persuaded us that cheering on others actually helped us—possibly even more than it helped the ones we were cheering for.

I'm going to turn the whole Ask discussion on its head (yet again) and suggest you tuck away your own questions and go out there and *answer* questions.

Not in the know-it-all way where you make people feel stupid but in a manner that makes them realize you want to help, that you put some thought into your answer, you could have also chosen not to have answered but you did and, hopefully, they benefitted from your answer.

In this way, we're on the other side of the coin (or fence or stadium).

We feel what it's like to answer the questions. We learn how much joy and pleasure we get from being helpful.

We also might learn how to ask better questions because now that we are answering them—and the pressure is off about whether or not we're formulating the question properly—we have a little breathing room and can answer casually and still succinctly.

Solve someone's simple problem. Well, something that was simple for you but not to them.

Cheer someone on who could use some encouragement. Answer their questions before they pose them. You know when that feels right and feels awkward. But try it.

Switch sides. Answer the questions.

We'll get better at asking them.

- **Possible:** Solve
- **Impossible:** Wait
- **Repossible:** Cheer

# 6

## SILENCE
DON'T EVEN ASK

"Just don't do it."

— The ad slogan Nike didn't go with

Asking can be difficult.

To ask means you're coming out of yourself, you're admitting defeat or lack of knowledge or at least that you're missing something and looking to fill it. Fill in your own blank as to what you're asking for.

It might be big stuff:

- "Please tell me what I'm doing with my life?"
- "Who am I?"
- "Why am I here?"

OK, so those were maybe too big. What if we tone it down a little.

- "Which path should I follow?"
- "What decision should I make?"

- "How am I going to get out of this \_\_\_\_ (job, marriage, rut, etc.)?"

Whew. Still pretty hefty. One more notch down.

- "Which project should I focus on?"
- "How am I going to make more money?"
- "When will I ever lose weight?"

I can't seem to get to the small stuff. I'm going to really try.

- "Should I have dessert or not?"
- "Tell my friends about it or make up a story?"
- "Share my question with my best friend?"

There you have it: asking can be a big deal.

**PLAN B**

Just don't do it.

Don't ask.

Keep it in, don't share, don't get the opinion of others.

If it stays with you, maybe it will go away.

If you don't share your questions with others, even close family or friends, maybe they'll stop pestering you about it.

Keep it to yourself for a while. See how that goes. Then maybe ask if you think they can help and you're at a point where you think you can handle the reality of it, or worse, their reality of your situation.

But for now, let's go with Plan B: Don't Ask.

This coming from a guy writing a book called Ask.

Just don't do it.

Hold it in.

Keep it to yourself.

It's easier that way.

For now.

Just get through today.

It'll be OK.
Things could be better but if we hold it in, maybe...
Maybe.

- **Possible:** Don't do it
- **Impossible:** Don't do it and say you did
- **Repossible:** Do it

## 7

# STEEK

STEEK JE VINGER OMHOOG

"The tallest blade of grass is the first to be cut by the scythe."

— Assyrian Proverb

*I* live in The Netherlands, I speak Dutch every single day with my family, colleagues, and, well, the rest of the entire country.

It's a thing here.

It's truly a part of who I have become and I even think in Dutch quite a bit.

Sometimes, a phrase will come to me sooner in Dutch than it will in English.

*Steek Je Vinger om Hoog*

"Steek" in Dutch can be translated into "stab" which gives it even more power. "Steek je vinger om hoog" means, literally, "stab your finger up." Another variation is "steek je vinger in de lucht" or "put your finger in the air."

In English, we say, "raise your hand."

All of it means you have a question to ask.

But I see it as a way to break through an invisible ceiling between you and the rest of the world.

Although I'm a native English speaker and "raise your hand" has a more visceral meaning for me, there's something about that pointy finger that makes it more powerful, sharper, and more...dangerous.

Because it's "dangerous" to ask questions. You'll immediately be "seen" in a sea of bodies not raising their hands. You'll be physically higher up as your hand goes up with your finger and even your arm is probably raised up as well.

But if you raise your hand (or your finger), aren't you the one who's going to be singled out? Won't you then be the one the spotlight is shining on?

Yes.

Then the question becomes: is that the person you want to be? Do you want to:

1. Stay at the same level of the rest (of the blades of grass, hidden in the lawn)
2. Rise up above to be seen, answered, and possibly...cut off.

Your cultural background can influence how you react to this quite deeply.

In The Netherlands, there's also a saying about how the tallest blade of grass is cut off. They're saying:

- "Don't stand out!"
- "Don't be unique!" and
- "*Doe even normaal!*" (Just be normal.)

There's an extremely common saying among the Dutch that goes:

*"Doe maar gewoon, dan doe je al gek genoeg!"*

Which translates into, "Just be normal, that's already crazy enough!"

This is the difference between not asking a question and asking a question.

It comes down to so much more. It's no longer about a question. It's about breaking through, rising up, and daring to be different or taller or the one with his hand raised.

Or your finger in the air.

It's up to you to choose.

It's up to you to choose what type of person you want to be.

To begin down the path to ask the question of *Who Will You Be Next?*

*Steek je vinger omhoog.*

- **Possible:** Be a blade of grass—like the rest of them
- **Impossible:** Pretend not to laugh at yourself trying to pronounce Dutch
- **Repossible:** Steek je vinger omhoog

## 8

## SAY NO

WHAT'S THE WORST THAT CAN HAPPEN?

"In any moment of decision, the best thing you can do is the right thing, the next best thing is the wrong thing, and the worst thing you can do is nothing."

— THEODORE ROOSEVELT

Although I've been studying the concept of asking for months and have read articles, interviewed people, and made it my goal to know the ins and outs of asking, we can't leave out the simple —and possibly most powerful—question:

**What's the worst that can happen?**

We all know the scene. We're in a situation where WE feel strong and at ease. Yet we're with someone who feels neither strong or at ease.

They are the ones who have to ask the question, however.

We coach them, prod them, motivate and inspire them to ask the question and we probably ask them 14 times, "What's the worst thing that could happen?" or in case you needed some fresh versions of the same question, you can use these:

1. If they say no, so what?
2. Is there any chance they will *murder* you for asking? (Insert favorite violent verb: maim, dismember, torture, pull your fingernails out, etc.)
3. Let's quickly analyze the statistics of asking: they might say yes, they might say no, they might even say maybe or next time or we'll see. That took 8 seconds and we have 4 out of 5 answers that are not no.
4. If you don't ask, you'll never know.
5. Maybe they'll have an answer you don't even expect, something beyond even yes, no, or maybe. They might come back with an even better idea beyond what you are even dreaming of right now.
6. If they say no, could you ask someone else?
7. Can you sweeten (or strengthen) the question before you ask?
8. Can you foresee (and/or study or research) all possible answers so you're best prepared for a follow-up question?
9. If they respond in the negative, do you have a response ready? Walk away, ask in another way, keep pushing, thank them and move on.
10. Could the "no" answer be truly worse than the "yes" answer?

I'm sure you have even more possibilities. Got a zinger? Something I'm not even thinking about? Want to share it with me/us? Come on over to the "What's the worst that could happen?" club at ask.repossible.com and add to the list of 10 I dreamed up in 10 minutes above.

See, I just dared ask you right there to break out of your comfort zone and initiate contact with me—and possibly a Facebook group of strangers who could possibly tear us all limb from limb for adding another one to the list.

Or you contribute and someone say, "Ooh, I like that one."

It's up to you.

- **Possible:** Answer badly
- **Impossible:** Answer the unasked question
- **Repossible:** Ask the question

## 9

# SUCKER

OH, YOU DIDN'T KNOW THAT?

"You're either humble or you're not. If you were a jerk before the fame, you just become a jerk with a bigger spotlight. Whoever you are really comes through."

— Oprah Winfrey

*A*s an author who has books titled "Play" and "Pass the Sour Cream," I admit I take things lightly and not much can get me down.

But I'm going to step out of my usually-ridiculously-friendly and encouraging and helpful self for a moment and go to town on people who do this thing. This thing that annoys me to no end.

Let me set the scene.

I'm going to make this up to highlight my point but I'm sure you'll recognize the situation and almost the exact words used to *sucker punch* you.

You're having a conversation with someone. It might be a friend but hopefully not because what they're about to do is something you don't really want to associate with.

They mention something, some fact or a name or a concept. Let's take something obscure, oh, I don't know, it could be as simple as a movie. Let's say, "The Green Mile."

The friend mentions the movie and let's say you don't know the movie. Still with me?

Maybe at that point you shake your head a little or shrug your shoulders or they ask if you know the movie or you state you don't know the movie.

Ready for the nasty part? Here it comes.

Then they *ask*, and they usually love to make this come out in very clear speech and they'll pause to make sure you heard it and will await your answer:

"Oh, you don't know the movie?"

— (Hopefully) Not Your Friend

They look at you, waiting for your response but what they're really doing is confirming you don't know the thing they were talking about and they do.

They are "confirming their superiority" over you because they have knowledge of this thing and you don't.

Ring a bell?

They clearly know you don't know the movie because you shook your head or shrugged your shoulders or said you didn't know the movie.

But then the repeat this "lack of knowledge" on your part to remind you of their superior status over you in the universe.

The really bad ones will repeat it again, often something like this:

"Oh, really? You really don't know the movie?"

— No Longer Your Friend

They sometimes nod a little and might even repeat the word "Wow." a few times for emphasis.

What's happening in their sheltered little minds is they are grasping at the chance to parade their brilliance and expose your ignorance in comparison to them.

These people are usually, well, let's make a quick list:

- Insecure
- Condescending (when they have the opportunity)
- Sad
- Not all that brilliant after all
- Bullies
- Maybe just clueless (about what they're doing)
- No longer your friends

When put into the position, you have several options. Most of them depend somewhat on how annoying you think this all is (and possibly how much more annoying you think it is now that I'm bringing it up and making such a point about it all…) and how much you want to keep this friend as a friend.

You can choose to:

1. Do nothing and let them continue.
2. Say something like, "No, I don't know that film." and let them continue.
3. Slap them lightly in the cheek and share this chapter with them.
4. Ask them if they have ever heard of an author named Bradley Charbonneau or possibly are familiar with a book he wrote called Ask and a particular chapter titled Sucker and when they say no, you can choose from the options above but ideally with the one that begins with, "Oh, really? You don't know him?" just for kicks.
5. An alternative to option #4 is to answer their question (about the movie) with another question about something completely unrelated and ideally more obscure you're pretty sure they won't know anything about and then go

through the whole dog-and-pony show of putting their "ignorance" on display preferably if you're on a stage or in a group of your peers—for added points.
6. Walk away and not explain anything.

We've talked about fear in this book. We've touched on the worst thing that could happen. We've had silence and wrong answers and dumb questions.

Each of us can choose how we treat those we interact with and we can be self-loathing jerks or we can lift up those within our reach any—and every—time we have the opportunity to do so.

Information and knowledge is not a finite resource. It's not a zero sum game.

You're deep into a book called Ask. You hopefully have learned a thing or two about how to ask questions, to dare ask them in the first place, to get over the fear of doing so.

Yet then comes along someone who is going to knock you off of your pedestal because you don't know a movie.

We have the choice to not be this person. We have the option to be a non-condescending teacher and uplifting friend or we can be that soul-sucking, sucker-punching person who, granted, perhaps even unknowingly, pushes someone down unnecessarily.

Now we know better.

We know the power of asking and the potential danger—and upside—of asking the right questions in the right way while avoiding the dumb questions in a condescending way.

- **Possible:** Sucker punch
- **Impossible:** Know everything—or even want to
- **Repossible:** Encourage

# PART III

# KNOW

"We know what we are, but know not what we may be."

— WILLIAM SHAKESPEARE

## 10

# KNOWLEDGE

WANT TO REALLY LEARN SOMETHING? TEACH IT.

"When one teaches, two learn."

— ROBERT HALF

My son and I are/were writing a book called, "7 Tips to be a Better Friend When You're a 15-year-old Boy."

Does he have a Ph.D in child psychology? He doesn't have a Ph.D in *anything*.

Has he read countless articles on the topic? I'm not sure he *can* read.

Has he interviewed dozens of teenage boys on the topic? Well, sorta.

How in the world is he an expert?

- He has good friends.
- He keeps them for a long time.
- They like him.
- He likes them.
- They have each other's backs.

Who is his book for?

For that teenage kids who wants to have better friends. Think those kids exist?

You betcha.

"But why," I hear you ask, "is he writing a book on it? Can't he just be satisfied with knowing something, being good at something, and call it a day?"

Aha! Of course he can.

But his dad is, well, uh, yeah, me.

I know that **by teaching something, by writing it out, making 7 chapters and expanding on your initial thought you learn, you learn it deeply.**

More than if you just sat there and recognized yourself as knowing something.

Plus, he might help some other teenage boys.

What if a teenage boy took one of his strategies and made a new friend?

Success?

Absolutely.

Now I know what you're thinking, my dear Toastmaster friends. You're thinking,

> "This is all really touching, Bradley, but I don't have–nor do I really want–a 15-year-old boy. How is this relevant for me?"
>
> — WHAT YOU'RE THINKING

Aha, here we go.

I have been asked to be the ambassador, the sponsor of a Toastmasters club in The Netherlands.

The club doesn't exist yet. The few founding members have zero experience in Toastmasters much less in forming a new club.

They probably don't know much about giving speeches, what to do with your hands, how to pause, how to move around the stage, how to evaluate the speech.

They probably don't know any of that.

Can you think of people who know that sort of thing?

Can you think of people who, in the eyes of those newbies, compared to those just starting out, have worlds of experience?

Here is my challenge to my club at Utrecht Toastmasters:

## Teach What You Want to Learn

What is something you would like to know more about with regards to public speaking? Is it more technical like timing or voice control? Or maybe a bit more nuanced like how can you connect with the audience better?

Want an extra challenge?

## Teach Something You Don't Know Very Well

Remember, you still know it better than that person who knows nothing about it.

All we really need to know is about 10% more than the other person to be of value to them.

If I were to pick a subject where I would like to improve, say, structure to my evaluations, I might:

1. **Sift** through my own knowledge,
2. **Talk** with others (especially those more knowledgeable than me),
3. Pay more attention to evaluators and **watch** how they work,
4. **Ask** questions, directly after an evaluation, to an evaluator about something specific I noticed.

Are you seeing what's happening? I'm paying attention. I'm learning. I'm asking. I'm getting better.

All because I'm going to Teach What I Want to Know.

This doesn't mean you shouldn't teach something you're good at.

When you do that, you just get even better.

We each know something more than someone else on the planet. If we don't know it well, we'll learn it before we teach it.

But in order to really learn it?

We need to teach it.

- **Possible:** Learn
- **Impossible:** Hide
- **Repossible:** Teach

## 11

# KIDS

### A LETTER TO MY 16-YEAR-OLD SON

"In fact, you couldn't give me anything to make me go back to being a teenager. Never. No, I hated it."

— J. K. Rowling

ear Liam,

You're 16. I'm sorry. It's such a tough age. Here's the conflict:

1. You're pretty sure you know everything.
2. You don't need any help with anything (see point #1).
3. You don't ask for help (see points #1 and #2).
4. You're good.

Maybe you'll read this when you're 26 (or 36…) and I don't even really want to give it to you anytime soon (see point #2 above).

But I'm going to write it anyway. Mostly because I'm your dad, I was also 16, I'm no longer 16, you are 16, and soon you will also no longer be 16.

But you are now.

I am here for you.
For anything.
For everything.
For anything and everything you want or need.

> **FUN FACT:** *There is a battalion of people around you who also want to help you, to answer your questions, to guide you to become a fulfilled, joyous, and happy person.*

But with them, and to some extent with me, you have to *ask*.

Sure, we can force "answers" onto you but if you're not asking, if you're not open to the responses (and don't really even want them), not only will they not penetrate your brick wall of resistance but we will eventually tire of trying to help.

Well, with the exception of your parents because we love you more than anything on the planet, we will continue to ask you questions and answer yours, and we will never tire of helping.

Here's the weird thing that is hard to understand at 16—which is why I wont' bother sharing this with you right now—but people genuinely want to help.

People truly love helping others.

We want to share our knowledge and if we don't know the answers, chances are good that we'll try to find them all in an effort to answer your question if only because you asked it.

But you have to ask the questions.

You have to allow people to answer, sure, that's important as well, but asking them is the first step.

If you ever think you are imposing on someone by asking a question or maybe you think you're going to look dumb or sound silly or just be a pain in the butt for asking, keep in mind that—careful, here comes a bit of math—usually the discomfort you may feel is inversely proportionate to the joy and meaning it provides others who you allow the opportunity of answering.

I truly feel like I'm now in paragraph two of your math word problem where I say the same thing in another way so you can answer the questions in the quiz but here goes anyway.

People in the world, especially those who are not 16-year-old boys, are actually waiting around for you to ask them questions, to seek their opinions, to open yourself up to learning and broadening your knowledge, and answering your questions.

It gives us meaning to feel that we can help.

It shows us love that you choose to ask us.

It showers us with tiny droplets of happiness that we can be a part of your life and perhaps influence the trajectory of your life in a positive way because we only, honest and truly, want the best for you and wish with all of our hearts that your life be full of laughter and heart-throbbing meaning and a purpose that makes the hair stand up on the back of your neck.

I know. You're 16. You don't think about this stuff. It might be a decade before you do. Maybe two decades.

But still, I'm going to write down "the answers" here even if you don't pose "the questions" just in case you're thinking of possibly asking at some theoretical point in the near (or distant) future.

But it's not just me.

It's anyone—and almost everyone—you come into contact with.

- Asking is power.
- Asking is love.
- Asking is growth.

This is going to sound strange, but asking the question is often the more important action than receiving the answer.

I know you know this part but asking the question is a whole heck of a lot more difficult, painful, and scary than answering it.

Which is exactly why I understand that you don't.

Which is exactly why I want you to understand that you do.

Could you do me one little favor?

Temporarily wipe away the fears.

Grapple over the mountain of nonchalance.

Quietly shed your armor of indifference.
It's just a three-letter verb.
But it's the most powerful tool you possess.
Just do this one thing.
Ask.

- **Possible:** Think you know it all
- **Impossible:** Know it all
- **Repossible:** Ask your dad

## 12

## KILLER
ASK AND YOU SHALL RECEIVE.

"We have to tell people who need help that it's OK to ask for it."

— MACKLEMORE

hy is asking so hard for so many of us? Let's get over it. Let's go over a few reasons we might not ask:

1. I've got this. Lone Wolf!
2. They're probably really busy.
3. It's going to take too long.
4. It'll be better if I just get it done myself.
5. I don't really even know what to ask.
6. I need to work on what I'm asking, make it more specific.
7. It doesn't really work. I mean, does it?
8. I did ask, but they didn't listen.
9. I think I asked, I can't remember.
10. OK, fine, I didn't ask. At all.
11. I don't know who to ask.
12. I don't really comprehend how much better it will be

when I get the advice or we work on it together than it will be if I go it alone.

The only legit excuse might be #6. Maybe sometimes #8, but not often.

I often write about topics where I need help myself. How else do you think I came up with all of those "excuses" not to ask so quickly?

The killer for me is #1 (probably why it came up first). It's related to #4. But #12 is pretty important and it's the main reason I'm writing this book.

The thing is I want to, ahem, ask others about their struggles with asking. See what happened there? I'm going to use my own fear/hesitation/lack of asking to finish up a book about how we can get better at asking.

Of course, you can go it alone. I've done it for years (if not decades).

Don't let the Lone Wolf kill your secret weapon of being strong enough to ask.

- **Possible:** Go it alone
- **Impossible:** Succeed alone to the same degree as with help
- **Repossible:** Ask for help

## 13

## **KEEP**

KEEP ON KEEPING ON

"Asking questions is the first way to begin change."

— Kubra Sait

*K*eep going. Keep asking. Keep answering.
Then ask some more.

It's like education or brushing your teeth or basketball: the more you do it, the easier it becomes and the better the results with less effort.

Asking is a mindset, a habit that we can build and grow like a muscle.

As we wrap up this first book in the series, I hope I have created a monster in you. A monster that has no fear of asking, no awkward silence when your questions aren't answered, and no shame in asking just about any question out there.

With the Dare book coming up next, you're going to need some ammunition, some weaponry, some power to get through that one.

That power is asking.

Now you have it.

See you in the next book: Dare.

- **Possible:** Ask one question
- **Impossible:** Ask two questions
- **Repossible:** Never stop asking

# AFTERWORD

What don't you dare ask?

    Have a question?

    Something secret thing you never came out into the open with? You can ask me and I won't tell anyone if you don't want me to.

    Isn't it weird like that?

    If you had asked me, many years back, but also over a span of many, many years, what "I wanted to be when I grow up," I probably would have lied or fumbled or mumbled or possibly said something about being a writer.

    I'm a friendly audience. I used to not dare ask. Now I always do.

    What do we really have to lose?

    Come over and dare to ask at ask.repossible.com.

# ACKNOWLEDGMENTS

If you're reading this far, I already like you. ;-)
    Whom do I acknowledge?
    How about you?
    There we go.
    I dedicate this book to you, the reader.
    The one who is going to dare ask.

# ABOUT THE AUTHOR

Bradley Charbonneau didn't used to ask much. He just did his thing and hoped it would work out.

It went OK.

This is Bradley's twenty-first book.

It is nowhere near his last.

*Ask, create, play at:*
bradleycharbonneau.com

 facebook.com/bradley.charbonneau.author
 twitter.com/brathocha
 instagram.com/brathocha

## THE END

This book is finished.
　　　　But you're just starting.
It starts with those nasty little three letters.
I dare you to ask.

REPOSSIBLE BOOK 4

# DARE

## TO ANSWER THE CALL OF YOUR FUTURE

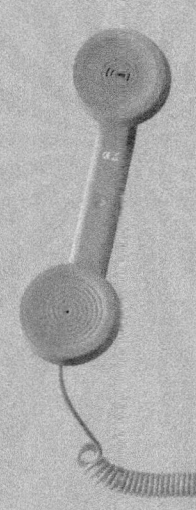

**BRADLEY CHARBONNEAU**

# PREFACE

Want to join us in building, growing, and molding what this book will become?

Or maybe even just watch a video of each letter of D.A.R.E. that might turn into:

- Do
- Adjust
- Receive
- Elevate

We're just getting rolling but come join us at dare.repossible.com.

"Far better is it to dare mighty things, to win glorious triumphs, even though checkered by failure... than to rank with those poor spirits who neither enjoy nor suffer much, because they live in a gray twilight that knows not victory nor defeat."

— Theodore Roosevelt

## DEDICATION
### FOR DADS, DAREDEVILS, AND DOERS

*And those who want to be.*
*Who dare to be.*
*Who dare to do.*

# PREFACE

"If you think you can do a thing or think you can't do a thing, you're right."

— HENRY FORD

Do you dare *answer the call of your future*?
There are generally two lines of thinking (and believing) when it comes to how much we humans can change over time.

1. **Fate:** we are who we are and that's that. Nothing or not much we can do about it.
2. **Choice:** we not only have a say in who we will become but we are an active player in determining our future.

Ha, I didn't mean to and I wish you could see me or I had a video of it but I just laughed out loud at myself as I type these words.
Because if I believed that first one, I wouldn't write this book. In fact, I might not write any books.
I'm a believer in the idea that we can change our personality, we can alter the trajectory of our lives (and we do so all the time), and we

can become someone who we choose to become. But there's only one person who can do so: you.

I'm a believer that we can fundamentally change who we are because I have done it myself. I went from dreaming of becoming a writer to becoming a writer.

I wrote those words with ease but that path was anything but easy.

I needed to *ask* and then *dare*.

1. We first need to *Ask* the big question: Who will you be next?
2. But then we need to *Dare* answer it.

This book will strive to help you dare to answer your question of you will become next in your life.

Ready?

Here we go.

# INTRODUCTION
## REPOSSIBLE

"It always seems impossible until it's done."

— Nelson Mandela

It was so clear.

Sitting on the steps of Union Square having a Chipotle burrito with John Muldoon.

"If you don't buy it in the next five seconds, I'm going to buy it," he threatened.

He said it nice but I knew he meant what he said.

I bought it.

Over the next few years, we talked about it but didn't take much action.

We *dreamed* and even *dared* but *didn't do* much.

We *discussed* and might have even *dabbled* in a bit of *design* but didn't get too far.

But it wasn't going away.

Lots of ideas come and go.

Most go.

This one wasn't going anywhere.

Until I took action.
Until I did something about it.
Otherwise, it would haunt me until I did.
The purchase went through and I just bought a name we couldn't believe was available as an exact dot com.
Repossible.com
It was so clear then.
It was often clear along the way.
It is so clear now.
It's Repossible.
Part of which you're holding in your hands.
The other parts are:

**Repossible**

1. Repossible
2. Every Single Day
3. Ask
4. Dare
5. Create
6. Decide
7. Meditate
8. Spark
9. Surrender
10. Play
11. Celebrate
12. Evaluate
13. Elevate

All under the larger idea of Repossible.
I dared to buy that domain, unsure of where it might lead or how long it might take. It was a gut reaction, a spur of the moment decision, and there weren't many downsides other than the $9 it cost.
Just that one word.

Dare.
What does it mean for you?

- **Possible:** Don't
- **Impossible:** Dawdle
- **Repossible:** Dare

**Dare Bonus Content**

Walking the talk of daring to do things I didn't used to dare do, I'm turning around the camera and hitting record.

I've always been a teacher at heart and I'm at home on stage. I love writing books but then I dive into deliriously delicious waters when I record the audiobook or a video.

In addition to this book, I have created Bonus Content, videos, audio, maybe there will be checklists or printouts, who knows what I dare do.

Maybe it will depend on what you dare ask me to create?

In any case, it's all available right now and I'll be linking to certain media directly from this book. You can start by heading over to dare.repossible.com and signing up. You'll get a few emails from me to introduce things and then you'll get access to the Dare Bonus Content complete with your very own user login and password.

Remember that first step? The one that "doesn't cost much of anything" except maybe a mouse click or $9 (repossible.com)? Yet the potential upsides are unknown, possibly fun, and potentially life changing?

I hope over at dare.repossible.com, that's one of the first steps in your path.

See you on the inside!

# PROLOGUE

o many verbs, so much time.

- Desire
- Dream
- Decide
- Do
- Don't

That last one is nasty.
Don't.
Don't do. Don't desire. Don't dream. Don't decide. Just don't.
Don't dare.
Want some even scarier verbs? These hurt. These are that "real stuff" that people don't like to admit, the stuff that gets whispered in back alleys, the "on my deathbed" kind of discussions. These are going to make this book 18+. Maybe I should classify it as horror. Here goes.

- Deliberate
- Delay

- Debate
- Drag
- Dwell

There are other verbs. I like these. They're fun (if sometimes a little scary).

- Ask
- Decide
- Create
- Spark
- Meditate
- Play

But none of them matter without that one:

- Dare

Dare to do that thing you haven't done.

**DISCLAIMER: don't do dumb dares**

We're not talking about jumping off the cliff into the lake. Not:

> "Dude, I dare you to dump that debris on that delegate from Dubai."
>
> — Dumb Dude

Not dumb.
Here, I'll give you one:
**I dare you to dabble in the dreams of your dares and delve into the depths of your delicious desires.**
I promise, I'll ease up on the use of the letter "d" word, just give me a few chapters to, ahem, drain it out of my system.

# FOREWORD
## BY BRADLEY CHARBONNEAU

I think it's customary to have someone else write your foreword.
   This book is called *Dare*.
   I'm going to write my own.
   As if I were someone else.
   Yeah, well. There you have it.

Foreword to Dare
   By Dakota Valentine

I always take the safe road. Not necessarily the easy path but the one that's going to work and I'm pretty certain is going to be OK.
   I'm partly wondering why Bradley asked me of all people to write the foreword to his book. But hey, I'm honored.
   If there were a fork in the road with a left, middle, and right, I would take the middle.
   The middle path. The safe way. The simplest, easiest, least potential for confusion or danger.
   It's working out for me. I get from A to B. I'm still alive.

But there's alive and there's thrive.

I'm not thriving.

I'm surviving.

No, really. I'm OK. I'll be fine. *Fine*. Nothing wrong with fine, right?

I'm good. "Hey, I'm great. How are you?" Seriously, all's well that ends well. That works. It does. No, I'm saying that. It's not a question. It works.

I'm here. I'm writing a foreword to a book. That's something, right?

Which path?

Middle road.

No detours, please.

I'll be fine, I promise. I might even be better than fine. You know, someday.

I'll get there. Want to join me?

Wow, as I read that last line, I would answer: *uh, not really. No thanks. You go on ahead.*

I think I need to read this book.

# PART I
# DO

# 1
## DO
THERE IS NO SUBSTITUTE

> "The best time to plant a tree was 20 years ago. The second best time is now."
>
> — CHINESE PROVERB

My dad passed away in 2015. I struggle sometimes to understand the idea in time that he'll never come back. The idea of never being the word I can't really comprehend.

In 2014, my boys were 8 and 10 when we "did that book project" as they like to refer to it. Never again will Lu (admittedly and voluntarily) write a little story about farting and aliens.

There is no way I could now get my 15-year-old-hair-in-his-armpits son Li to sit down a record a chapter of a book he wrote and followed through with it until it was right.

But frankly, I got what I wanted. What I have today is the audio of each boy reading their own chapters. It's priceless. Of all of the *Side Effects* and *Benefits* of this entire operation, those two audio files are what I cherish most.

They'll never be 8 and 10 again. In fact, it was only during that year.

This section is called Do.

It's one of those "Wait, that's way too simple." kind of things. They hurt because they're true.

You do or you don't.

If you need a time element thrown in for good measure, here you go.

*It's now or never.*

Just a hint but "never" sounds so vague, doesn't it? "When does that happen, actually? When does never exist?"

Yeah, roll around with that one in the hay.

- **Possible:** Delay
- **Impossible:** Defer
- **Repossible:** Do

Want a video version of this chapter? Here's your first introduction to Pepper, my office in the woods, and where I think most clearly: Dare Do the Difficult Deed is at dare-do.repossible.com.

## 2
# **DREAM**
#### BUT THEN AWAKE

"A dreamer is one who can only find his way by moonlight, and his punishment is that he sees the dawn before the rest of the world."

— Oscar Wilde

e're still early on in this book. Maybe I should have added a little disclaimer:

"If you don't dream, if you don't dare believe or think or wish or even want a better _____ (life, existence, meaning, you get the idea), then this book probably isn't for you."

I remember growing up hearing:

"Go to school, get a job, retire, get a watch, go on a cruise, and die."

I guess I just didn't feel that was really meant for me.
I wanted adventure and the unknown. Danger and risk and who knows what. Unexpected. Magic.

Dreams.

Sure, there are crazy, way out there dreams. Those are fun. But I mean more the kind we can actually achieve.

You have those, right?

I have lots. I think I might have too many. I don't know, can we have too many?

Again, not the stuff we'll seriously never achieve (star on an NBA basketball team).

But I don't know, write 17 books. (Yes, this is my 17th book.)

There's a good example.

Why?

Because just a few short years ago I had zero books. Then I started writing (see intro about John Muldoon—he started me writing right around the time we bought Repossible).

I kept writing.

I wrote one book.

The rest were easy.

No, really.

But I had to have the dream first. A direction.

Dare to dream.

You don't have to tell me—or anyone—about your dream but you might want to take a little action towards it.

Or a lot of action.

Dare.

Dream.

∽

## Dede

When she was 50 (give or take), her kids were off to school and she thought, well, OK, fine, I'm going to put words into her head:

"Get busy living or get busy dying."

# Dare

— Andy Dufresne, in The Shawshank Redemption

Some people see a certain number, be it 40 or 50 or 60 or 70, and they think:

"Well, I guess that was about it. I'm pretty much done here. I can just get out the remote for the TV, find my favorite slippers, and wait until ... "

— Bee Naught Yu

An aunt of mine was, well, I don't know how old, but she just threw in the towel. She decided she was done and wanted to be old and taken care of. She didn't have the energy or the drive or the will or I don't know what she didn't have but she didn't have a dream—or at least not a dream that took much asking, much daring, much creating.

Yet Dede didn't quite see it that way.

I don't know if she did the numbers in her head but if you calculate and guesstimate you'll live until, oh, I don't know, 81 and you're 51, that's 30 years. Thirty years. 30 x 12 = 360 months or around 10,800 days.

Do you remember when you were 0 years old? Of course not, your brain was functioning like an iguana. How about when you were 5? 10? Maybe at 10 you have some memories?

What if you saw 50 as 0?

How's your memory? Sure, you might joke that you can't remember what you had dinner last night but WHO CARES what you had for dinner last night? No one. Not even you.

What you could or should care about is what you're going to do with the 10,799 days you have left to live your life.

Oops, missed one. Oh yes, that's because I'm not counting today. Today already started.

So, what's it going to be? I smell a numbered list of questions.

1. Get busy living
2. Get busy dying

There's usually a choice. It's usually yours.

- **Possible:** Dread
- **Impossible:** Duck
- **Repossible:** Dream

## 3

## DEADLINE

"THIS IS ONLY GOING TO HURT A LITTLE."

"A goal is a dream with a deadline."

— Napoleon Hill

**W**hat else do they say at the doctor's office:

"This is going to hurt me more than it hurts you."

"There's going to be a sting."

"It'll be a quick pinprick and then it might burn a little but then the worst will be over."

### Set a Deadline

Choose a date. In the future. Go ahead, make it far into the future. It doesn't even really matter when the actual date is.
 It's more important that you set it.
 In stone.

Do they have stone calendars? They should. Then we could set the date in stone.

We'll have to settle for digital. Or paper. Or you could even write it on a wall or desk calendar if you have one of those.

But we need to make it real.

## Real Deadlines

We all know about fake deadlines. They usually fall under the broad umbrella of diets and "other things we're not really going to do."

"I'll start working out on January 1."

Here's a crazy idea: set a deadline for when you'll stop instead of start.

"But when do I start?"

## Option 1: Right This Very Moment

Right now. Today. Right this very minute.
Start now and choose a date to stop.
It takes away that whole future element and removes any question of when you'll start.

> **PRO TIP:** Today is a whole lot easier to figure out than "Pick a Day, Any Day." Oops, dang it, that's the next of the next heading.

## Option 2: Pick a Day, Any Day

Let's narrow it down. Make it this calendar year. If you're in the late fall, say, October 17 or later, you can also choose the first half of next year.

But choose a date.

I chose November 17, 2019 for the launch of this book. It is October 14, 2019 right now as I write this.

Think my book is done?

Nope.

Think I'm working on it today because I have a deadline of a month from now?

Yep.

Pick a date.

Share it with us at facebook.repossible.com.

I won't tell anyone.

Oops, I just did.

You just did.

See how good that feels?

"This is only going to hurt a little."

You'll feel better almost immediately.

Once the swelling subsides.

Feel better already?

That's because it's now *real*.

## Liam

October 31. It's his birthday. He'd be 16. At 16, in The Netherlands, you can ride a scooter.

It was spring. He calculated the money he needed to buy one—or at least half if we were to gift him half for his birthday.

He looked into which jobs you were legally allowed to do under the age of 16.

He walked into a local supermarket and asked about a job. He got an interview. He was on time. He got the job. He worked the maximum number of hours he could legally get—and balance with school.

He saved. He worked. He had a deadline.

October 31 arrived. He had the money. He did the research on which scooter and where and how much. He narrowed it down. He made phone calls. He learned about Marktplaats (like Ebay).

He made an appointment. We went together. Everything was in order.

He got his scooter.

It started with a deadline.

- **Possible:** Delay
- **Impossible:** Dive back in time and do what you didn't do
- **Repossible:** Deadline

## 4
# DON'T
YOU DON'T HAVE TO DO THIS

"The man who rows the boat seldom has time to rock it."

— Bill Copeland

*D*on't rock the boat.
Don't change. Don't do. Keep the status quo.

It's an option I don't want to overlook. You don't have to do this. You don't have to do anything (well, there's death and taxes, I suppose).

When someone is pulling you in a direction you don't want to go, you don't have to comply.

I want to make sure that here in a book called "Dare" I offer of the option of not daring. Or rather, to dare not to dare.

### Gern

There was a turning point in Gern's life that he brilliantly maneuvered and prevented a life he may or may not have loved.

The road less traveled, as it's often called, consisted of leaving his friends and family and everything he knew for an international existence that sounded great in novels and magazines but just wasn't what he wanted to do.

He wanted to stay near where he grew up and build the friendships that would last a lifetime. Truly get to know people in a way that's only possible after years if not decades.

He could still travel, he just didn't need to go and live in all of those foreign countries for years and years.

Sure, he might give up learning other languages and meeting people from around the globe but in this way, he also built up a solid group of friends.

They go on annual ski trips and every other year do a bigger trip with just their close-knit group.

He knows where to get his shopping done, has a short list of people he knows well to go to in any situation from a leaky faucet to strategic financial advice to where to retire.

He doesn't have to deal with all of the hassles of living far away from home and balancing visiting family with creating a new life wherever he ended up.

He doesn't have to establish new friendships and probably lose them when he moves again.

He doesn't have to do. There was an option to not do and he chose to not do.

By choosing to not do, he's choosing to do something else.

So maybe there is no "don't" it's only a choice and that choice is yours.

Gern chose the life of not doing what some thought he should do and doing what he thought was his right to choose to do—or don't.

- **Possible:** Don't
- **Impossible:** Don't and say you did
- **Repossible:** Do it even though you don't feel like it or want to succumb to the doubters who don't dare do what you're dreaming of doing

# PART II
# ADJUST

## 5

# ADJUST
## YOU'VE STARTED THE RACE

"When it is obvious that the goals cannot be reached, don't adjust the goals, adjust the action steps."

— Confucius

You can't edit nothing.

The coach can't help you if you don't show up for practice.

A teacher can't estimate your talents if you don't give her a taste of what it is you can do.

But once you begin, after you take that first step, when you finally give up, give in, and change your mind to go forward, then we can adapt your pace, alter your path, and adjust what you have begun.

- **Possible:** Wait until it's perfect but then do it before it's perfect
- **Impossible:** Wait until it's perfect (which means never)
- **Repossible:** Adjust

I went to record a video for this chapter but I forgot my tripod. Guess what I did? Find out at dare-adjust.repossible.com.

## 6
# ASK
I HAVE A QUESTION

> "You begin a film more with questions than with direct intentions. It's more of an exploration and discovery."
>
> — ALEXANDER PAYNE

*I* have a direct question for you:

**What have you dared do?**

I'm looking for opinions, experiences, discussion, and, can I find another "d" word...*dialogue*.

Sure, I have plenty of thoughts on the verb "dare." Here I am starting a book about it. **That** is daring.

But that's my MY definition, my experience, my ideas.

What are yours?

If you're waiting for someone to ask you, here's me asking.

bradleycharbonneau.com/asking/

My work, my books, my pretty-much-everything has gotten better since I've opened up to, you know, those other humans who live on the planet for their interpretation of things.

*They* meaning *you*.

Your stories, your experiences, your opinions.

What do you say?

Here's my pitch:

- 15 minutes
- On the phone
- No guarantees
- No requirements
- Just talking about the verb *dare*

Maybe we don't get anywhere, maybe we end up talking about Indian food (which is not a bad thing…).

Maybe we find one tiny nugget in our 15 minutes of conversation that merits its own chapter.

Maybe it's an entire section.

Maybe it starts with the letter d…

I digress.

A short time ago, I wouldn't have dared ask you to talk on the phone with me for 15 minutes. I was scared. Of what, I'm not sure but those are the worst fears: the ones we don't really understand.

Dare to have a chat?

bradleycharbonneau.com/asking/

**Editor's Note:** OK, fine, Author's Note: I'm not sure this is clear but this chapter is extremely daring of me. I'm putting a link in here for you, dear probable stranger, to hop on the phone with me. I mean, that's just plain crazy, isn't it? Sure is. A short time ago, I would have never done such a thing. I'm becoming more daring as I do more partly because I ask, "What's the worst that could happen?"

∾

## Gwyneth

Anyone can ask a question. Still, most don't. Sure, they answer lots of them, but they don't ask them. Then they don't do the next even more important step: listen.

Gwyneth sits back, listens, waits, almost like a lion in the savannah. Except she's not going for the kill. She's waiting for the next question to ask.

She might do a little chit chat, a bit of friendly banter, but at some point, she's going to pounce and attack.

Her "attack" is a bite into your core. She comes at you with the real questions, the kind that make you think and, almost wish she didn't ask.

Why not? Why are you scared?

Because she sees through the fluff and dives right into the heart of the matter. She doesn't have time for "news, weather, and sports" and what makes her day, what turns her eyes sparkly and warms her heart is asking the good questions, the tough one, the kind that make you think, often bow your head in thought (or defeat), and then rise up and do the bold thing: answer.

- **Possible:** Ask only when you know the answer
- **Impossible:** Ask yourself and never others
- **Repossible:** Ask

## 7

# AIM
### THE RIFLE VERSUS THE SHOTGUN

"Aim for the moon. If you miss, you may hit a star."

— W. Clement Stone

Niche down. Focus. Niche again. Narrow your reach. Ready. Aim. Fire.

Or just shotgun it and hope you hit something.

In the writing world, there are two types of authors:

1. Plotters
2. Pantsers

**Plotters** plot and plan and make blueprints and follow them.

**Pantsers** "fly by the seat of their pants" and create and make and do and then see what happens.

Another set of labels that might be easier to understand is:

1. Architects
2. Gardeners

See note above about blueprints for the architects but as for the gardeners, this is the moniker I like best:

*"spread your seeds and see what grows"*

I'm a card-carrying pantser/gardener.

I'm also the first to admit the benefits of the plotters and architects.

I also fully believe that consistency and "confinement" breed creativity.

The first section of this book is Do. It's not Aim (or Focus or Sit Back and Think About It for a While).

It's Do. It's action, creating, making, and yes, then see what happens.

This book is called Dare. In earlier versions, I had a purple cover with a man puking up a rainbow into a cloud. (If I were really daring, I'd put that cover at the end of this chapter...)

This book isn't called, "Safe Strategies to Be Boring."

- Act then aim.
- Create then analyze.
- Do then adjust.

I thought about putting "Aim" before "Do" but I thought about where to aim for too long and I wasn't doing.

That was a gardener joke.

You see, I need to first do in order to aim. That might not be you and that's OK. But you have to do one of the two things:

1. Do and Aim
2. Aim and Do

If you'd rather aim first and you feel strongly about it, awesome possum. In fact, dare you tell me about it? Remember that invitation? It's still open: bradleycharbonneau.com/asking/.

Did I warn you that this book might pull you out of your comfort zone? I just invited you to tell me why you'd rather aim before doing.

I also just opened up the possibility that you might actually do it.

I took aim below on a version of the cover of this book. Yep, it's a purple cover with a guy puking out a rainbow.

Pretty weird, right?

But it's how I saw Dare for quite a while.

Barf up anything and everything and then examine it, improve on it, see what happens.

How much worse could it be than a purple dude puking rainbows? It can only get better, right?

## Tom

"We need a new driveway," Tom announced.

Before anyone could say or do anything, Tom went to the garage, picked up a sledgehammer, went over to a corner of the driveway and started smashing the concrete until he had broken up a good chunk of it.

He started. He made progress. He took the first steps.

The next thing that happened was nothing.

He didn't take it further. He didn't even smash up some more concrete. Nothing happened.

Yes, he took action. Yep, he started all right.

But he had no plan, no follow-up, no nothing at all other than that very first action.

Now, concrete is hard and difficult to put back together in a way that looks like it has been untouched. Nope, he sure broke it up. That first day, he was determined!

The corner of the driveway lay broken up in pieces for a few years. An eyesore. A reminder that he didn't have a plan, that he acted without aiming, he started to build without a blueprint.

The broken pieces were representative of ideas started but not finished.

Finally, years later, he hired a company to build a new driveway.

He became more hesitant to just "jump into" projects without a plan. He became a little less adventurous.

But not completely.

There was still the element of action and surprise, of just "doing without thinking" but he became smarter about it and thought it through at least to the point where it wasn't going to physically break things and be irreparable without the help of professionals.

If you're ready to go, you're on the edge of your seat and you happen upon a section of a book called "Do" and the author is egging you on to just get started, think about the consequences.

- Will there be broken pieces lying around for years?

- If you do begin, can you easily finish?
- Is the project bigger than you can handle?
- Is it not the worst idea in the world to first aim and then act?
- Or is it a case where acting, where doing, is the right thing to do first and you can aim later?

It's not a cookie cutter solution and beginning a book is not the same as laying a new driveway.

Choose your battles.

If I had to give any concrete advice (pun intended, thank you very much), it would be this:

1. Pick up the sledgehammer and think about it.
2. Pick up the pen and write.

Although the pen can be mightier than the sword, the pen doesn't usually leave the pathway to your house in broken shambles.

- **Possible:** At least give it a go, no, wait a while, OK, fine, get started
- **Impossible:** Get it absolutely perfect every time you start something new
- **Repossible:** Aim, Ready, Do

## 8

# **ALLY**
### TEAM UP AND THINK EXPONENTIALLY

"Talent wins games, but teamwork and intelligence wins championships."

— Michael Jordan

After the initial "do" of the first part of this book (and the first step in your action), allying with a team or partners is possibly the most difficult yet also the most rewarding and important aspect of *dare*. In fact, that simple idea is the foundation under Spark.

Maybe in the Ask chapter, you dared step out of your comfort zone and asked others for advice or help. Awesome possum.

But when those conversations and meetings and phone calls transform into collaborations, partnerships, and even friendships is when things can really take off.

You have come out of your shell, maybe even out of the closet from where you were hiding with your idea or plan or identity.

You find like-minded souls and care to ask if they want to partner in something. Start small, get a feel for the fit. Date before you marry —but do date!

If you've read any of my other books, you'll know I can't get too many chapters in without at least mentioning math.

I often talk about simple equations that help me understand the meaning on a deeper level.

For example:

$$1 + 1 = 2$$

Simple addition.

The thing is, I believe in abstract math where:

$$1 + 1 > 2$$

You and someone else are together greater than the sum of the individuals on their own.

The biggest challenge for me to get over was I was opening up my "brilliant ideas" to someone else and, gulp, maybe they're not so brilliant to someone else.

You know what happens more often that not? Those brilliant ideas can get even better with the input and third-party perspective of someone other than yourself.

Expand beyond yourself. Go past just what you think and know. Ally with others.

∼

Dear Reader,

These two concepts, Ask and Dare, are possibly two of the hardest, most challenging, threatening, fear-inducing, would-rather-eat-paper, let's-just-not-do-this-and-say-we-did actions I bring about in any of the Repossible books.

Later on, with books like Surrender and Play, we're at a higher level, things are fun, light, even funny. Woo hoo!

But back here? In the beginning? We're neck deep in the actions where most of us stop: asking the tough questions and daring to answer them.

Here, let's do a really nasty one.

"Who will I be next?"

In other words, you are who you are now but if you'd like your future self, your better self, your dream-life self to make an appearance anywhere but in your dreams, you're going to have to ask yourself if you're willing to make the effort to take the steps to make that happen.

Then you're going to have to dare answer them and do what's necessary.

I write this here because **This Is The Hard Stuff**.

Yep, here I am an author with a whole bunch of books now. Ask me how long, how many years, how many decades I didn't dare ask "Who will I be next?" because I was scared of not even becoming that person.

How long did it take me to dare ask for help from others? How much did I regret not daring to ask for help when I learned how much people like to help others?

Ouch.

Yep.

Pain.

Suffering.

I add this comment here not to give you an excuse but to tell you that I've been there, I've done that, I've done this.

I've not asked.

I've not dared.

Which is why the previous book was titled **Ask**.

Which is why this book is titled **Dare**.

It's the hard stuff.

I wish it were easier.

If it were easier, everyone would do it.

You're not everyone.

You're you.

It's time to ask yourself: "Who will I be next?"

Then ask, "Do I dare answer?"

But what I hope, what I implore, what I wish I had known so many years ago is that it's all easier, it's all better, it's all more fun and rewarding with you do it together.

This little chapter called "Ally" here in the Dare book, seemingly insignificant yet so powerful, is the key to rocketing ahead faster than you'll get there on your own (that is, if you get there on your own) and if there's one place where I hand out *Big Ideas* or even *Big, Juicy Secrets* buried in books, it's this: Ally.

— The Author

## Corinne

Corinne and Caryn partnered up for their new product. Each of them is brilliant in her own way and, yep, each could have done the job separately.

On their own, they wouldn't have to deal with phone calls and meetings. No discussions and setbacks because they couldn't agree. On their own would have been easier and maybe a bit more efficient.

But together?

Together they shine. With the two of them, they highlight each other's strengths and fill in one another's weaknesses.

They are a team. They can go in together on a more challenging phone call with a potential partner and tag-team their answers.

They form a cohesive unit that is learning to work together and they both are learning from each other in ways neither expected.

They get new ideas, different directions, and they have both learned to accept that their way might not be the best way but if they make their case well enough, it might be the way they go.

With a discussion. Maybe a quick phone call.

Together.

Ally.

- **Possible:** Go it alone
- **Impossible:** Go it alone and reap the benefits of being better together
- **Repossible:** Spark the energy in someone else

# PART III
# RECEIVE

## 9

# **RECEIVE**
## LET IT GO, LET IT IN

"Whatever we are waiting for - peace of mind, contentment, grace, the inner awareness of simple abundance - it will surely come to us, but only when we are ready to receive it with an open and grateful heart."

— Sarah Ban Breathnach

For those of you to whom the "R" section of this book might need a more strong or uplifting or even *difficult* verb, let me introduce you to the concept of receiving.

In part one, we *did*.

In part two, we *adjusted*.

We have *done* quite a bit already. We have given out, we have created or made then we altered and adjusted.

This may seem like the time to push harder, to *take it to the next level*, to strive and jump higher, give it your all, really go for it.

Yeah, you could do that.

But there's a point when you need to sit back, relax, and **let it come back to you.**

Think of a boomerang. You have thrown it, it is in flight, it's doing its thing.

It will return. It will be heading your way very soon. You have done your deed and it needs a little time to settle.

My 16-year-old son wants to cook pasta in half the time at twice the temperature. It doesn't always work like that.

Things need time to simmer, to let the juices sink in, to take a step back and see it from afar, from a less action-oriented perspective.

Let it out. Let it go. Don't worry that it won't come back. After parts one and two, it will return whether you like it or not.

While it's away, think about it, relish the idea that it will return but you don't have it back yet, plan what you'll do when it returns.

Open your arms, broaden your ideas, let it come to you and be ready to receive.

- **Possible:** Give
- **Impossible:** Give, give, give and think you'll receive without consciously doing it
- **Repossible:** Receive

I'm in the woods again (PRO TIP: I'm always in the woods) and I'm walking through how to receive. It may sound odd but many of us don't do this enough and/or don't even know how to do it. I know I was guilty for years of not letting it come to me, not accepting, not receiving. Catch some woodsy video version of receiving at dare-receive.repossible.com.

## 10

## REFRESH
UNPLUG. WAIT FIVE MINUTES. TURN IT BACK ON.

"When you are creating to the magnitude that I try to create, your brain is like a computer, and you need to refresh."

— MISSY ELLIOTT

Most technical challenges can be solved with the "just unplug it for five minutes" solution.

Many human challenges can be solved using the same technique.

Part one (Do) probably took quite a bit of energy.

Part two (Adjust) might have even taken more—even though we think part one is the hardest.

Unplug.

Leave it alone. Let it sit.

Let it come in. Allow it to come to you. See it from a fresh perspective: *refresh*.

I know what we need.

More "R" words.

- Reload
- Relax

- Rehearse
- Repair
- Reset
- Restore
- Resolve
- Respond
- Retry

Ooh, here are a few nasty ones:

- Regret
- Resuscitate
- Revive

Let's stay away from those.

Gee, there are lots of under the letter "R" are those with the *re-* prefix. Here's what dictionary.com has to say about that:

> *re-*
> *a prefix, occurring originally in loanwords from Latin, used with the meaning "again" or "again and again" to indicate repetition, or with the meaning "back" or "backward" to indicate withdrawal or backward motion:*

**Again and again.** We thought we were done "adjusting" in part two.

We're never truly done adjusting. We learn from doing over and over. Refresh is such a powerful word here because it gives us both that freshness of seeing something new even though it might not be new but also like hitting the refresh button on the keyboard and expecting it to be changed, altered, updated, edited and then when it does change, when the cache is cleared and the freshness arrives because we don't stop, it's *refreshing.*

The good stuff rises to the top, usually becomes easier, more natural.

The bad stuff sinks to the bottom and sticks to the pot. We can scrape it away later.

It's time to grind it out to the point where it becomes a part of you. It's time to *rehearse*.

- **Possible:** Hit refresh on the keyboard without having made any changes behind the scenes and see changes
- **Impossible:** Just keep hitting refresh and hoping
- **Repossible:** Refresh: make the changes, refresh the screen (and your experience) and see it in a new light

## 11

# REHEARSE
### 95 PAGES OF CRAP

"Practice doesn't make perfect. Practice is perfect."

— Bradley Charbonneau (from "Every Single Day")

*L*ook at that! I'm quoting myself in the headings of a chapter. Ha.

I just got off the phone with an aspiring author. She asked me how I write so much.

My answer was easy: I write every single day.

No excuses.

I practice therefore I get better.

If I practice *better*, I get even *better* even *faster*.

We could get into the whole math equations how "anything multiplied by zero is zero."

In other words, you can't improve on nothing. You have to have something to improve on.

In part one, you dared to do. Awesome: you now have something to work with.

In part two, you adjusted, improved, maybe analyzed a bit.

Now you have something better. Probably.

Write it out. Speak it through. Whatever it is you're working on, do it again and again.

You'll get better. There will be bad rehearsals. Good. Get them out of your system.

> **PRO TIP:** *you learn more from your mistakes than from your successes. If you keep messing up, unpack it, analyze it, figure out what you're doing wrong and fix it. Then do it again and again fresh.*

You know what's not so fun?
Rehearsing.
Why?
Because it's not "the real thing." It's just a trial run, an attempt, a practice game, a rehearsal.
*Pretend it's not.*
Make your mirror your audience.
Turn that one reader into many.
The hairbrush into a microphone.
You know what you're almost ready for? What you're practicing for?
You're just about ready to…roar.

## Steph

My 13-year-old son is good at basketball. He's a huge fan of the Golden State Warriors' Stephen Curry.

Steph is known to shoot another 100 3-point shots after practice. Did you catch that?

1. The main practice is over.
2. The rest of the team is heading for or already in the locker room because they have rehearsed already, they're done.

3. He stays.
4. He does more. He *rehearses* more.
5. He exceeds what he's supposed to do.

Why?

Because he wants not only to be better—those in the locker room are all better than most—he wants to be *his* best.

Note I didn't say *the* best but *his* best.

We can't concern ourselves with others when we're rehearsing. We focus only on ourselves and how many rehearsals will it take until it becomes natural, second nature, until it becomes not just what we do but who we are.

- **Possible:** Hope for the best that you get it right the first time
- **Impossible:** Get it right the first time every time
- **Repossible:** Rehearse even when you don't feel like, when you know it's good enough, just give it that one more round

## 12

# ROAR

### LET THEM HEAR YOU DOWN IN THE VALLEYS

> "I am impelled, not to squeak like a grateful and apologetic mouse, but to roar like a lion out of pride in my profession."
>
> — JOHN STEINBECK

*I*'m not really a *roar* type of guy. I don't go the hilltop and yell at the top of my lungs to celebrate my success—or cry out my loss.

I'm more of the whispering lion.

I write a sentence (maybe even a paragraph...) that I think is the bee's knees (I've also never used that phrase in my life but let's roll with it here, I might be onto something) and I feel the roar in my heart.

It's also in my gut.

Quite literally.

Like butterflies.

You do feel them.

Here we are in the third part of this short book yet let's do a quick recap:

1. Do
2. Adjust

If you have done #1, you're already ahead of most of the living population. Another book in this Repossible series is called Create and I don't hold back about how important I think creating (or doing or making) is.

Take a look around you. Earbuds in, eyes glued to screens, drool going unnoticed as the zombie apocalypse waits for the metro.

If you take that first step and "do" something, make a thing, write a paragraph and that was a big deal for you, let me know about it (facebook.repossible.com) because then do you know what happens?

Then I'll be rooting for you.

Do you know what happens when someone has got your back, when they're on your side, when they rejoice in your advancement?

You have a team. You have momentum. You have "we" instead of just "I."

If you haven't done or started or acted, head back to chapter one and take action. Then come back here.

Let's recap, it's just so fun.

**Do. Adjust. Roar.**

Celebrate the small successes. Pop the cork on the first step you've taken. Toast the tiniest moments of progress.

Roar with delight. Roar with pride.

You have it in you.

Maybe it's quiet like mine but it's there.

We just need to let it know it's OK to be heard. Even if no one hears it, this roar, this celebration is for you. It's important and one of the reasons I put it in here is because I'm not very good at it.

> **PRO TIP:** I don't write books because I know everything. Each chapter is not a huge success where I have conquered some

challenge. Far from it. I write books, well, for the most part because I can't not write them. I'm addicted to writing. But aside from that, they say that you should write books you want to read. I need to learn how to roar more. I need to celebrate those small successes and I need to do it more often.

As I write words, as I fill chapters with knowledge from me but mostly from others and their experiences, I'm taking notes. I'm writing to help myself and give me a path at least as much as I'm writing for you.

**AUTHOR PRO TIP:** Are you an author? An aspiring author? Maybe more along the lines of, "Ooh, I'd love to write a book someday but…" Please take this into consideration. You don't need to be the all-being master of the subject. All you really need is a passion for the subject, some experience with it, ideally some really bad experiences and then maybe a few successes.

Then you share with others who are heading down a similar path in hopes that your experiences can help lessen the downsides of theirs and increase the upsides.

See? We're in this book called Dare and I'm trying to remain out of my element and share things I might normally hold back for fear of being … (choose your favorite fear).

I'm daring.

I hope you are, too.

— The (lack of…) Management

Back to the chapter now after that note inserted from "The Management." Where were we? Oh yes, roaring.

If you need that quiet mountain top, get up there, look around, warn the birds, and let it rip.

Or let those butterflies have at it.

But whatever you do, celebrate.

Roar.

- **Possible:** Roar once in a while. Like a mouse.
- **Impossible:** Never, ever celebrate.
- **Repossible:** Roar to the world, to friends, but at least to yourself. Do it as loudly or as quietly as you like.

# PART IV

# ELEVATE

## 13

# **ELEVATE**
## TAKE IT UP A NOTCH

"Take a chance! All life is a chance. The man who goes farthest is generally the one who is willing to do and dare."

— DALE CARNEGIE

*I*f you've come this far, you're dared to *do* and *adjust* and *receive*, let's go all the way and *elevate*.

A later book in the Repossible series is called Elevate. But let's touch on the topic.

Let's say you're at Level 0 of whatever it is you're doing. You'd like to get to Level 1.

At that point, Level 2 or Level 47 seems incredibly difficult and far away and probably near impossible.

You first need to go from 0 to 1. True.

But once you go one level up you might look back and say:

"That wasn't so hard."

— YOU

Let's say you struggle to get from 0 to 1 or 1 to 2 or at any level. At that point, you might look back and say:

"Wow, that was hard."

— You

Either way, you went up, you ascended, you rose, you elevated.

Remember way back in Roar? How I was commenting about how I don't do it enough? Celebrating? Elevate plays a similar roll for me.

The book you have in your hands was one of the first of the Repossible series. In fact, it existed before the series existed.

Did you catch that?

There was this book (and Ask) but there wasn't a series yet.

Because I kept at it, because I believed in my message, because I didn't give up, it grew into something bigger.

Sure, Dare on its own is important. Dare to answer the big questions and all that. But it's even more powerful when the whole playing field is lifted.

If Dare is a game, a match in an entire season, it's an important one, but it's part of a bigger picture.

Yet had I not dared to write Dare then Repossible might not have ever made it into existence.

Are you following me here?

Let me make it super clear and believe me, I'm typing these words right now as both an author and a reader because I need to be reminded of the wins and how **daring to do could lead—does not always lead—to higher levels.**

Here's a bit of a spoiler for the upcoming book Elevate: when you get to what you currently consider the end or the finish line or the grand finale, it's only the beginning.

You'll do it all over again but at a higher level.

Here's a really bad analogy: you go through your entire high school career to graduate and cheer and be full of pride only to then do another four years at university.

Can you see how sometimes we might not want to keep going?
Yet, Repossible, Ask, Dare, Create, Elevate.
We'll get there, we'll want to get there, we'll get there together.
Then we'll go even higher.

What did the guy say about the thousand steps? Something about how it still begins with the first one?

Elevate.

- **Possible:** Keep plodding along at the same level for a really, really long time.
- **Impossible:** Stay at the same level forever. And ever.
- **Repossible:** Elevate one step at a time but take the step.

I dared ask my son hold the camera and film me daring to elevate at the sand dunes in the woods right here: dare-elevate. repossible.com.

## 14

# EMPTY

DOES EMPTYING ONE BUCKET FILL ANOTHER?

"Don't die old, die empty. That's the goal of life. Go to the cemetery and disappoint the graveyard."

— MYLES MUNROE

*I* was just talking with a friend I hadn't seen in 15 years. We went to business school together in Rotterdam.

He said he turned around his life when his mother passed away.

I replied that I turned around my life when my father passed away.

So it's *possible* to "turn around our lives."

But it often seems to "need" an **external event** to spark it into action.

Do we *need* the external event?

If we do, could we replace the family member dying (or the doctor's news or the boss's new plans) with something internal?

Can we decide to "repossible that" without the aid of an external force?

And if not, can I offer you the spark of Repossible to kickstart the life you wanted to lead?

"Disappoint the graveyard."

That's got to be one of the best "life mantras" I've ever come across.

## Periwinkel

Per didn't say whether or not his mother directly or expressly or openly held him back.

It might have been subconscious. It might never have been said or hinted at or even whispered in his youth.

But when his mother passed away, something was jostled loose within him and he was free to become who he was holding back from being.

He and I both agreed that it would have been nice to have had this *message* a bit earlier and not waited around for someone to leave this earthly plain in order for us to take a step towards the people we knew we wanted to become.

If you're reading this and you have even the slightest inkling that you might *die empty* if you don't do what you need to do, please don't wait for someone to pass away or for a prognosis from the doctor or some other life-altering event.

Alter life yourself.

Take charge, be proactive, and alter life before an external factor alters it for you.

Don't die empty.

Disappoint the graveyard.

- **Possible:** Wait for the disease or the death or the life-altering event (usually of the negative variety) before you dare to take action
- **Impossible:** take action with no internal or external event

- **Repossible:** Don't wait for the external event (to change internally)

## 15

## EDUCATE

WHEN YOU TRULY WANT TO LEARN, TEACH

"Education is not the filling of a pail, but the lighting of a fire."

— WILLIAM BUTLER YEATS

This is the section where I explain how to do it.
I have talked with lots (no, really, way too many) of people about Spark. Often when I get into the How of it all, they'll say:

*"But it's easy for you to say, you've already done it."*

Let's do some more examples, just for kicks:

1. The marathon runner runs marathons. (Because he's already in shape.)
2. The brain surgeon does brain surgery. (He studied it and, hopefully, has had lots of experience performing brain surgeries.)
3. I have written 5 books with my kids. (Because I got that first one started and done.)

Did I just put myself in a bullet list with marathon runners and brain surgeons? Absolutely.

They all had a Day One. That day when they knew nothing, couldn't do anything, were beginners.

After my MBA, I was a Management Consultant. The big secret behind management consulting is that you just need to be one step ahead (or off to the side) of the client.

**We teachers only need to be one step ahead of our students.**

Sure, it can often help if we're several steps ahead of our students but sometimes, they can relate to us better if we're not all that far ahead of them.

We're in the Elevate section. That means we have risen up—even if ever so slightly. Still, you're above someone who didn't rise up.

This might sound crazy, but "educating" others can lead to even more education on your part. I'm fully convinced teachers often learn at least as much as their students.

Here we are in Dare. In the Educate chapter.

You have dared to do something (or will soon—like when you finish this book). Share that experience with someone who hasn't yet dared.

I doubt they'll say this but they could say—and I write this so you'll be ready for it:

> "What do you know? You've only done it once. You're just one step ahead of me."
>
> — Them

Just one step ahead?

Ask about that one step to the person:

1. Who came in second in the 100-meter dash at the olympics

2. Who fell into the snake pit whereas you got your footing on the last solid rock
3. Who needs that hand outstretched from someone who just did it, who just completed what they have been trying to complete for a long time

That person is you.
You have an opportunity to educate, to lift up, to bring them up.

**SECRET SAUCE:** My mother-in-law taught me this but there is more joy and meaning and happiness in giving than in receiving. My mother taught me there is more joy in teaching than in learning.

You may consider yourself a student but you're already one class ahead of the one who skipped out.

- **Possible:** Wait until you're a certified expert in the field
- **Impossible:** Wait until they ask for help (from an expert)
- **Repossible:** Give, teach, and learn even more—and do it soon, like, now

## 16

# ESCAPE

DIP YOUR HEAD UNDER THE WATER AND LISTEN

"Once we accept our limits, we go beyond them."

— Albert Einstein

*I* have a clear vision of the word escape. Maybe it's because I'm an author, a fan of words, a lover of turns of phrase.

But I'm also terribly visual. To a fault. I "see" things in line charts, in IMAX-quality visions, and I do my best to describe them in words —if we're in a book, which we are here.

It's often a room or a conference center or something like a concert hall. There are lots of people in seats and it's like a bowl with the sides rising up, sometimes quite steep.

Again, I don't know, I don't "see" these things on purpose or consciously, they just come to me, but we float or rise to the top, just like a helium balloon would do.

There at the top, we find a portal and we can easily open it. We pull ourselves through (gravity isn't quite doing its thing at this time) and we're out.

We're up in the sky or the clouds or space or…whatever it is that means escape for you.

From here, we lie down on our stomachs and look back down into the hall. We can often see ourselves (or our old selves) down in the hall. We can see clearly and yet also from a higher perspective. So both a wide-angle lens and a zoom lens—but at the same time.

We can see clearly.

We observe, listen, and quickly and silently learn what we need to do, how we need to think, where we need to go from here.

This is the place above from which we can make better decisions, to dare or not dare to do the thing, and it's easy from up here and we know why we decide what we do.

That's it. That's often my escape.

**The Ocean**

If that visual doesn't work, have you ever been scuba diving or snorkeling?

When you're floating on the surface of the ocean, ideally a calm place, you see the sky and hear the wind and the waves but once you put your head under water, it's a different world.

But no, really, truly, and clearly a *different world*.

It sounds different—there are bubbles we hear and squeaks and squawks.

It looks different but even how we see it. Probably through a face mask and things might be magnified or zoomed in or out.

Fish and critters swim around you. If you poke your head back above, nothing, none of this seems to exist but you pull your head back under and it's all right there—you can touch it—or try.

Two worlds and you're in the middle of them. You're right there at the border and you have access to either and both. Just with a lift or drop of your head, you're in both, you're a part of them together and yet separately.

Escape.

Two worlds, both accessible, both clearly in existence, and you have the key to both right there, right now.

You choose.

Later in the Repossible series comes a book called "Meditate."

Meditation is the water-free version of this that is accessible to you all the time without need for face masks.

What was that quote from that guy at the beginning of this chapter? Oh yes, that's right, something about limits.

"Once we accept our limits, we go beyond them."

— Albert Einstein

Accept your limits.
Go beyond them.
Escape.

～

### Andy

Andy wanted new books for the prison library. He wrote a letter every single week to the city library asking for donations.

After a long, long time, he he got a response and they succumbed to his incessant banter.

They sent him some books.

But rather than rest on his laurels and declare victory and stop with the letters and *quit while he was ahead,* he saw that he had broken through a glass ceiling, he had ascended to a point never before reached, and this was the sign to him that he could go higher.

Rather than see the dip under the water of the ocean as the victory, he saw it as the entryway, the portal to another dimension or world or level and then he made his move.

He didn't just dunk his head under, he took a deep breath and dove into a whole new world that opened up because he took the action, he stuck with it, and made it happen.

"From now on, I'll write two letters a week instead of one."

— Andy Dufresne in *The Shawshank Redemption*

He didn't just "keep going" but he doubled down and went all in.

> **SPOILER ALERT:** *After two letters a week for a while, the library donated more books, money, and an expansion of the library.*

If you don't feel like you should be where you are (like Andy in jail), can you escape? If you can't escape your current location or environment, can you escape in another way? For example, through Meditation or Creation?

Escape is a daring chapter of the section called Elevate because it's going way higher to the point where it doesn't seem like it's part of the same world.

Which is because, often, it isn't.

Dare to escape once in a while.

- **Possible:** Watch movies of people escaping
- **Impossible:** Wait until you're in jail to plan your escape
- **Repossible:** Escape into levels beyond what you even previously dreamed of elevating to

# AFTERWORD

"Gamble, cheat, lie, and steal. Let me explain: Gamble for your best shot in life - dare to take risks. Cheat those who would have you be less than you are. Lie in the arms of those you love. And finally, steal every moment of happiness."

— Caitlyn Jenner

I gambled for my best shot.
　I dared to take risks.
　I cheated those who would have me be less than I am.
　I lay in the arms of those I love.
　I did it.
　Now I'm doing it.
　Now what about you?
　My book is here. It's done. You're holding it in your hands. Check!
　I'm interested in your change, your dare, your hurdles and doubts.
　I'm taking it to a place I call "Beyond the Book" where I have quick session videos, audio, and things you can't do with words on a page.

You can check it out from the back row. You can sit in front and ask questions.

You can take the mic and sing me a song.

You have to be open to the change.

Then waltz on over and say hi.

If you haven't joined us yet, come see what's going on at dare.repossible.com and/or join the Repossible Facebook Group at facebook.repossible.com.

# ACKNOWLEDGMENTS

If you're reading this far, I already like you. ;-)
   Whom do I acknowledge?
   You.
   I acknowledge you.
   For daring to be you.

# ABOUT THE AUTHOR

I think there are two levels of daring.

1. Internal
2. External

It may seem at first that the external dare (in public, with strangers, on the Internet) would be scarier, more difficult, and full of excuses.

But it's the internal dare that is the bigger mountain to ascend.

I overcame that particular internal dare when I accepted a challenge to write Every Single Day on November 1, 2012.

Through overcoming the internal dare, the external dare (coming "out of the writer's closet" and going public with my dream of becoming a writer) became easier, not really even an issue, and just went with the flow of following through on the internal dare.

Since 2012, I take up dares on a regular basis. I closed down my design agency, I moved my family to Europe, and I'm writing, teaching, and speaking full time.

Because I accepted the challenge of an internal dare to strive towards the person I believed I wanted to be.

I currently live in a little town outside of Utrecht in The Netherlands with my wife Saskia, famous two young boys of "The Adventures of Li & Lu" fame, and our at-least-as-famous dog Pepper.

This is my seventeenth book.

It is far, far, far from my last.

*Find, ask, discuss, play, and dare at:*
bradleycharbonneau.com

facebook.com/bradley.charbonneau.author
twitter.com/brathocha
instagram.com/brathocha

**THE END**

*I* dare you to not dare.

REPOSSIBLE BOOK 5

# CREATE

WHAT TO DO WHEN YOU DON'T KNOW WHAT TO DO

BRADLEY CHARBONNEAU

## DEDICATION
### FOR THE CREATORS

*No, not THAT creator.*
*People like us.*
*Who make stuff.*

*But mainly for Tony.*
*Creating until he was 105 years old.*
*Probably holding art workshops in heaven.*

"There are basically two types of people. People who accomplish things, and people who claim to have accomplished things. The first group is less crowded."

— Mark Twain

# PREFACE
### CREATE.REPOSSIBLE.COM

I'm an author. Yep, words onto pages to make books.

However, this book is not called "Write," it's called "Create."

In my books, I mention November 1, 2012, quite a bit. It's the day when I started writing. You know, actual words onto a page. Like *real* writers do. Just like I'm doing here. Unless you're listening to the audio version of this book and then it would be spoken words into your ears.

The difference was, up until October 31, 2012, I hadn't been writing. I hadn't been doing much "creating" at all.

Sure, I thought about it. I dreamed about it. I even talked about it sometimes at parties as something I was "going to do someday."

Do you know what I'm talking about?

It's so easy to talk about what we'd like to do rather than do the thing we've been talking about.

But now it's some seven years later.

On November 1, 2012, I took a *seemingly insignificant*, 30-day writing challenge and wrote all 30 days. Then I hit 100. Then 1,000. Now I'm at something like 2,749. No. wait, I can calculate, this book, my 23rd book, will arrive on "Create Every Day" number 2,783.

**But now it's not just writing. It's creating.**

You see, what happened was that I became a writer, an author. **I become something I didn't think I was ever going to be.** It pained me to no end to think I would never be a writer.

And now I am.

Now I feel like I can do whatever I put my mind to.

I can *create* my own future.

I have (and will still...) gone through many subtitles of this book. One of them could be:

**I can create my own future.**

You might want to say *design* my future or maybe *plan* or even *forecast*.

Nope, *create*.

Once I realized I had actually become a writer, something happened.

I gained confidence. I had a system. I could do anything.

Other dreams popped up. Dreams and plans I had long hidden away because if I couldn't manage to become a writer then I could simply forget that *other stuff*.

That *other stuff* being:

- **Speaking** (on stage, to schools, to audiences, improv)
- **Teaching** (courses, workshops, retreats)
- **Narrating** (audiobooks, podcasts)

The reason I mention this is my creations have gone far beyond words on a page.

**create.repossible.com**

I'd like to welcome you to come over to create.repossible.com where we'll enhance these words here with video, audio, interviews, case studies, and even mini-courses all based on the ideas in this book.

I'm going to be linking to specific pages within that domain so if you'd like to head over there now and sign in, then you'll be logged in for each link and it should then show up immediately.

You see, now that I've started creating, I can't stop.

It's an addiction.

But the good kind.

I think they call those *habits*.

I have a *daily creating habit*.

It's what I wish for you, too.

- **Possible:** write a regular book with words on pages
- **Impossible:** deliver an in-person workshop
- **Repossible:** go all out with recorded video, audio, quizzes, and gorgeous downloads

Although I'm not a huge fan of reading books on my phone, I'd like to think this book is more of a performance made up of words, both written and spoken, video, images, sounds, birds in the background in the woods, even dogs in the foreground, and an experience for you to experience with your earbuds while on a walk and maybe sitting down on a bench to read another few quick chapters.

# INTRODUCTION

> "A journey of 1,000 miles begins by making sure the parking brake is disengaged."
>
> — BRADLEY CHARBONNEAU (*MY RENDITION OF SOME NEPALESE GURU'S FIRST STEP OF 1,000 STEPS IN SANDALS...BUT MODERNIZED*)

*Create* has so many elements and angles to it, there's just so much here and so much to say and...

Did you catch that?

All of these ideas, this *content*, these creations and here I am, the author of the book titled *Create*, going to *Walk the Talk* and follow my own *Constraint Breeds Creativity* chapter to tame the beasts, corral the cats, and lay down the law of the land.

> *Because, at the end of the day (well, frankly, at the beginning of the day, but we'll get into that later...), you have so much to create, so much to give, say, do, and make that you'll wonder how you ever kept it all inside.*

My business partner would laugh as I write this word but here comes something rather scary in my life:

**Structure**

I do an exercise with each (nonfiction) book where I take the main word or idea and spell it out and find verbs (or adjectives, but usually verbs) that begin with that letter.

For Create, it became:

- **C:** Challenge
- **R:** Repeat
- **E:** Educate
- **A:** Amplify
- **T:** Trust
- **E:** Evolve

But there were all kinds of verbs:

- **C:** Change, Claim, Connect
- **R:** Raise, Receive, Reflect, Release, Relish, Reveal, Roar
- **E:** Echo, Empower, Engage, Erupt, Escape
- **A:** Abandon, Accumulate, Adjust, Align, Allow, Answer, Ask, Astonish
- **T:** Tap, Test, Tickle, Turn
- **E:** Envisage, Establish, Explore, Extend

So we're going to go on a bit of a journey.

We'll start with **Challenges**, both action related and mindset shifts.

From those beginnings, we'll want to **Repeat** our steps, see what works, then do more of it.

We'll be learning along the way but there is passive learning (as in, "I learned so much from that Netflix series over the past 9 days!")

and then there is **Educating** yourself where you take what you learned and apply it to the next step.

We're now into something of a mini flow state where we're repeating what we started with, we're learning from it and it's time to turn up the heat, step on the gas, and **Amplify** our power.

We're cruising now. We're on the highway of creation and we're feeling good, making progress, and, wait, did we miss an offramp? Were we supposed to be on this road? We're going to need to **Trust** the process, allow ourselves the benefits of the doubt, and go with it.

Yep, we're on the right road—or at least the road we're on is the road we're on—and it's time to elevate, turn on the after burners, take off, turn our car into that space-age vehicle and **Evolve** into a higher level of creation we probably didn't expect to come along so soon—if ever.

That's a sketch of the roadmap of our *Create* journey.

So buckle up, grab a snack, and put on your traveling hat because we're about to *Create*.

# FOREWORD
## BY SOMEONE ELSE

My dream is to have this written by Joanna Penn.
She said:

"I measure my life by what I create."

She also has a hand-written notecard which reads:

"Have you made art today?"

She has a photo of herself holding up the card and you can see her eyes behind it and she looks like she's waiting, expecting, even encouraging or challenging you to answer the question.
It's here:
https://twitter.com/thecreativepenn/status/908163704327458822

# "BOOST YOUR BRAND WITH A BOOK"
## FROM "INVISIBLE IMPOSTER" TO "EXPERT ENOUGH"

"Every entrepreneur should self-publish a book because self-publishing is the new business card. If you want to stand out in a world of content, you need to underline your expertise. Publishing a book is not just putting your thoughts on a blog post. It's an event. It shows your best-curated thoughts and it shows customers, clients, investors, friends and lovers what the most important things on your mind are right now."

— James Altucher

Here you are, just getting started with a book called CREATE written by a guy who has written 26 books and you might, be saying to yourself after finishing this book:

"This dude goes on and on about CREATING, but what should I create?"

— You

OK, maybe you don't say "dude" when you talk to yourself, but you might be thinking about me writing all of these books and wondering how I do it.

Here's the thing.

**I honest and truly want everyone on the planet to write a book.**

I believe it's therapeutic, it brings magical ideas into even the dustiest of brains, and, the best part: *it opens doors.*

Writing a book, especially if you have a business or you offer services or you do ANYthing that you charge more than $2.99 for, is always a smart business move.

Why?

Because a book is still regarded as a "high value" item. People respect you more if you write a book. They take you more seriously and if you have a business and you wrote about a topic related to your industry, you are, immediately, an "expert in your field."

I hear you saying:

- "Bradley, I'm not an author! I can't write emails properly!"
- "Bradley, I don't have time to write a book!"
- "No one would read it."
- "It would be terrible."
- "A book? I'd love to. My clients would love me, but I don't know what to write about."

I get it. I've been there and I've done that.

Let me cut to the chase.

The easiest way to write a book is to not do it alone.

I can tell you because I've written books alone (not so fun) and written them together with others in groups with deadlines and collaboration and accountability (way fun).

I have teamed up with an awesome partner. Nicoline Huizinga is a visibility strategist so her job is to get people visible. Guess what makes her clients more successful? If her clients have a book! Can you imagine what would happen if you had a book for your business?

Consider this:

1. more (online) speaking gigs,
2. more participants to your online courses and
3. more 1:1 clients you could work with.

Because people have seen or read your book—and they want you in their world.

Nicoline and I are running 6-week training program where we are going to work together with you to get your book from idea in your brain to a book on the (digital) shelf in 6 weeks.

Not 6 months, not 6 decades, not 6 lightyears.

6 weeks.

From idea to shelf.

I know you're a creator--or want to be a better one (we're ALL creators, we just need practice)--that's why you have this book in your hands and why you're still reading here in the 29th section before the book even starts. ;-)

So let's get down to business.

Our courses are not just "watch these videos and good luck with that." We have weekly group calls, co-working hours, accountability moments, and a (private) chat group. But most of all, we have others in the class who all want the others to succeed.

If this sounds like something that could get you from "invisible imposter" to "expert enough" and get your book idea from inside your head to on the page, check out our program here: bbb.repossible.com.

Oh, one last thing.

Because you're a CREATE reader, you can use this discount code to take 25% off of the price of the course--and any other course at Repossible.

The code is:

CREATE

Of course. ;-)

OK, now get back to this book and get creating!

I'm rooting for you.

Bradley

# PART I

# WELCOME

"I shall create a new world for myself."

— Frederic Chopin

# 1

## ARE YOU WAITING FOR SOMEONE TO ASK YOU?
### HERE'S YOUR INVITE

> "A real conversation always contains an invitation. You are inviting another person to reveal herself or himself to you, to tell you who they are or what they want."
>
> — DAVID WHYTE

*I* was waiting. Then someone asked me. Now I'm asking you.

Do you want to do this? Maybe you're a little hesitant? I don't know, you're at least this far into this book.

Have you been waiting for someone to ask you directly? Has it not happened? Are you still holding out for that cinematic moment when the sun is setting, the beer bubbles are still coming up from the bottom, you sigh, take it all in and know this is your moment.

Wait for sunset.

Grab a drink.

Because I'm going to ask you.

Your invitation is waiting for you at create-ask.repossible.com.

Just in case you're someone like I am, who sometimes just needs to be asked even though they know they want to go, they want to do it.

Just checking that box.

- **Possible:** analyze
- **Impossible:** assume
- **Repossible:** accept

## 2

# BOUQUETS OF FLOWERS, MEN IN SUITS, SOMBER FACES

### THIS IS NOT GOING TO END WELL. OR WILL IT?

> "When you're happy you find pure joy in your life. There are no regrets in this state of happiness—and that's a goal worth striving for in all areas of your life."
>
> — SUZE ORMAN

*It* was time.

It was Thursday morning. I was out front wiping the dewdrops off of my son Luca's bike seat before he went to school.

Across the street were three cars. Well, three cars more than normal.

Young men I didn't know came out from the back gate with way too many bouquets of flowers. They were wearing suits.

A woman had an elegant evening gown on. But it was 8:30 in the morning.

They gave me courteous waves. I waved back.

I saw my neighbor. She saw me. She's one of the sweetest people I have ever (barely) known.

You know those types? You don't really know them well but you know they are good, warm, genuine.

That's her.

Her husband had some bad medical news a few weeks ago. Seems like it may have turned for the worse.

They all drove off, Luca's seat was well dried by now, and our dog, Pepper, was hoping we'd go for a walk.

In other words, life goes on.

For some of us.

I don't pretend to have all of the answers. Just some of them. Some that have worked for me.

If I were the one whose life they were celebrating that morning, would I be OK with it? Am I ready to go? Have I done here what I wanted to do?

No way.

But I have to admit: over the past short few years, I'm a whole lot closer.

The secret?

**Create.**

My wife said to me this morning as she was getting ready for work that she has been missing San Francisco lately (we lived there for 17 years).

> *"Maybe it's because I have a job now and I'm back in the daily grind."*
>
> — MY WIFE

Now it wasn't terribly appropriate to bring up my *The Big Answer to Life's Mysteries* at 7:18 in the morning to my wife who is (how do I put this delicately?), not exactly a morning person.

But I have a *Big Answer*.

**Create.**

I believe we're all creators.

I believe we need to create stuff. Make things. Build, draw, write, compose, do.

Where there was nothing and now there is something.

It doesn't mean it has to be commercial. We don't all need to be best-selling authors or famous composers or oil painters. It's not necessarily even about being an "artist" except that artists are such clear examples of people who create.

But we all need to create.

We need to get it from inside to the outside.

What is it?

Whatever it is you have inside that wants to be outside.

Let's take my neighbor.

Want to ask him what he has left with the world? Yep, it's morbid, but he can no longer answer.

What do we want to create to leave behind?

Or let's get those morbid thoughts out of the way for a moment.

1. What do we want to create right now?
2. What's holding us back?
3. Why aren't we doing it?

I can think of a host of reasons to not do it.

1. Fear
2. Judgment
3. Time
4. Priorities
5. Focus
6. Clarity

Enough? Does anything resonate?

What if you were attending the funeral today of my neighbor. You might have one of those moments where you think:

"Gee, if that were me, would I be OK with it? What might I have done differently?"

— You (at my neighbor's funeral)

Do That Thing.
I don't mean to say that we're all creative.
Oops, scratch that.
That's *exactly* what I mean to say.
We are all born creative. We just allow other stuff to get in the way.
I hear you now. You're asking.

"OK, Bradley. Let's say I buy into your message here. Great. But what do you want me to do?"

— You saying to Me

**Create.**
Make something. Do something. Turn a thought into a thing. Create something.
It won't be judged, there is no fear, no one is watching.
Well, except for the future version of yourself.
What does that future self want? What would they advise you to do right now?
When I have an idea that won't go away, I write about it. Can you tell I'm working on a book called ... *create*?
When I see things simply and clearly yet I can't quite get the full power of the message across it usually means I need to write more about it.
Did you catch that?

**I don't need to:**

1. Learn
2. Research
3. Take in
4. Consume.

**I need to:**

1. Write
2. Revise
3. Think
4. Let it out.

I have to stop.
I have my idea.
It might not be clear to you. Yet.
But if I had the solution to all of life's problems? We're down to one word.
**Create.**
If you want extra bonus brownie points, here's an even more powerful word although this is for the advanced class:
Co-Create.
I've turned "co-create" into a simpler word: <u>Spark</u>.
Are you ready?

- **Possible:** wait
- **Impossible:** hide
- **Repossible:** create

Oops, just in case this isn't all completely clear, this is what we're going to dive into in this book.

## 3

## HERE TO CREATE
WE'RE NOT PUT ON THIS EARTH TO WATCH TV

"There are two great days in a person's life: the day we are born and the day we discover why."

— WILLIAM BARCLAY

*I*'m just going to cut to the chase:

**We're Here to Create**

We're here to make stuff. We're here to get what is inside of us out into the world.

I don't mean we all need to be full-time painters and live in an atelier in Paris and drink Four Roses Bourbon (although that was fun...).

But we need to create.

We *need* to.

Well, that is, if you want to thrive, to rise up, to get off of the plateau we're often stuck on.

It doesn't have to be fireworks and mayhem. No marching bands and orchestras lifting our spirits.

It might be a short story. It might be a drawing. It might be, in the secrecy of your car after work on the side of the road, a minute of a dialog of a character you have in your head--that one who wants to be set free.

We all have them. We can suppress them or we can set them free. We set them free, we set ourselves free.

We're here to create.

I wanted to put this chapter here, complete with this photo, to show a real example of when we're working on something, the *rest of the world works together with us*.

Not only are we here to create, but when we create, others see it, notice it, cheer us on, and support us.

Well, for the most part.

There are also those who will be envious, jealous, and maybe even try to sabotage your progress. They are jealous. They are not creating themselves.

But when you're creating, the world comes to your aid, it shows up unexpectedly and makes it known that you're on the right track.

Just like when I saw this poster.

It works just like that.

When you create.

- **Possible:** see it
- **Impossible:** ignore it
- **Repossible:** allow yourself to soak it in and relish it

## 4

# LIVE, WORK, CREATE. PICK ONE.
### WHICH ELEVATES THE OTHERS?

"Get busy living or get busy dying."

— Andy Dufresne (in The Shawshank Redemption)

*I* suppose you could do the whole, "You're on a deserted island." thing but how often do we really find ourselves on a deserted island?

**Live. Work. Create.**

Quick Quiz: if you could only pick one?

How about more along the lines of:

1. You're in your life.
2. The one you're currently living.
3. Yes, that one.
4. No islands.
5. No deserts.
6. It's now and you have a choice.

That's going to take care of **live** if we're down to one. We're going to live the life we want to live no matter what. Oops, except that it might not be working out as well as we had hoped.

Speaking of working out... We can just toss **work** because, I mean seriously, who put *that* in there anyway?

What are we left with?

**Create.**

I wrote a book called Dare—I'm getting better at *daring* to make bold statements. I'm going to dare go out on a limb here and dare, challenge, and rock the boat by saying that to **Create** is a more important action than to **live** or to **work**.

There, I said it.

Maybe it's because I write every day. Maybe because I can't not write. I have it in my system, in my blood, as part of who I have become.

*If I'm not creating, I'm not living.*

Some people might call that work. Maybe that's how that word got in there.

**Work** is stuff I have to do (pay bills, figure out how software functions, etc.).

But to **create** is to **live**.

It might be an idea, a plan, even a holiday planned.

It's something you used your mind (ideally that imagination section) to make something that wasn't there before.

But a physical thing (yes, a book, a painting, a song) is easier to see and understand and accept as a symbol of that thing you now did.

But it doesn't need to be physical. It could be a thought that becomes a project, an idea that turns into a business, a _____ that develops into a _____. You fill in the blanks but it's nothing that becomes something and the difference is the action you took.

Create.

What does it mean for you?

- **Possible:** work
- **Impossible:** live
- **Repossible:** create

I just created this chapter. Is it going to win an award? Probably not. Did it intrigue you? Pique your interest? Get you thinking?

Then it was worth it for me to have created.

Oh, and if it didn't do any of that for you, it might the second time around or as you read these words right here because I'm now actively engaging you in this discussion.

# PART II

# CHALLENGE

"The ultimate measure of a man is not where he stands in moments of comfort and convenience, but where he stands at times of challenge and controversy."

— Martin Luther King, Jr.

## 5

# HOW WILL YOU DEFINE SUCCESS?
IS IT ALL DOLLARS AND CENTS? OR MAYBE SCHOLARS AND SENSE?

"Success is steady progress toward one's personal goals."

— Jim Rohn

*A*ccording to Jim above, "steady progress" is it, it's the goal, it's *success*.

So, let's see here, if we just keep going, we proceed, we make progress on a regular basis, then we're succeeding?

Yep.

That's exactly what he's saying.

This is exactly what we're saying here.

The marathon isn't the goal. The training is the goal.

Let's list a few more stereotypical markers of success:

1. Money
2. Fame
3. Power

Recognize those? What if we measured by a different scale? What if success were measured by things like:

1. **Passion:** got some of this? It's going to be useful later on in this book. If you don't have it, we'll get you some.
2. **Practice:** the marathon runner is "successful" because he has a practice. What if we measured by the practice and not the goal?
3. **Persistence:** it's not just 3 days and done. Persist with the practice and the *success* will come. Oops, you'll find out soon this *is* the success.
4. **Patience:** maybe it arrives on Day 17. Maybe it's week 17. Relish the process.
5. **Productivity:** with passion, practice, and persistence, we're going to be more productive. This, in itself, is success.
6. **Potatoes:** sorry, I was on a roll with the "P" words and that's what came through. Maybe I'm just hungry…
7. **Meaning:** the daily practice will give you meaning in your life. No, really. Yes, it's that simple.
8. **Purpose:** when you're down the path a ways and you look back at the meaning you've built up, you may have just stumbled upon your purpose.

Can you think of more new measurements towards your new success? Let's walk though it in 7 minutes in the woods right here in this video at create-success.repossible.com.

- **Possible:** compare
- **Impossible:** succeed
- **Repossible:** get a new ruler

# 6

# WHAT IF YOU DON'T KNOW WHAT YOUR PASSION IS?

## LET'S GO GARDENING

"A seed depends on a whole host of factors to grow - from the fertility of the soil to the right mix of rain and sun to not being eaten by a passing bird. The same goes for an idea. For an idea to really take hold, other factors come into play, from timing to the emerging technology that makes it possible."

— TAAVET HINRIKUS

If you don't know what your passion is, how are you supposed to follow it?

Sure, I write books like "Every Single Day" but what if you can't figure out what you're supposed to do all those days?

You're more than willing and even able to do it, but you don't know what to do?

You want to do it--but you're not sure what it is.

How can you find it?

In the video at the following link, I turned on the camera and in a matter of 12 minutes, I found a better way of trying to get across what I had at the beginning create-passion.repossible.com.

- **Possible:** watch grass grow
- **Impossible:** harvest (before you plant)
- **Repossible:** plant a seed

I'm going to give away "the big secret" of where to find your passion right here in case you don't get to the video above.

- **Seed:** plant seeds (take (conscious) action). See what grows. Not all will take. Nurture what blooms.
- **Meditate:** sure, you'll get some ideas and inspiration (at least, I hope!) from my video, but the answers are within. Let them out.
- **Wing it:** I can wholeheartedly recommend what I did in the video above: turn on the camera, press record, go.

## 7

## VIA NEGATIVA
LET'S GET RID OF A HABIT

"Negative way" or "by way of denial"

— Latin meaning of via negativa

We're early in this book still so let's take a moment to "make some room."

By creating, we're probably adding something to your daily life. We'll later get into what exactly you'll be doing or making or creating but chances are you might say, "But I don't have time for this."

Which is why we probably need to get rid of something to make room for something new.

We have 24 hours in the day. Every single one of those days, we have the opportunity to choose what we'll do with that time.

We can't make more (or less) of the minutes and hours but we can remove some of things we do to make room for new ones.

We're in a book called Create. I can tell you right now it's going to take some action on your part.

Sure, we'll get into areas where you'll learn how to create "while doing something else" but you're going to need at least a little bit of "newfound" time to get things rolling.

If you can, right this very second, think of something you can give up or stop or at least temporarily put on hold for the next month or so, great.

If you need some help, here's a quick list of things we do that we could either stop, slow down, or at least take a break from to add in something new.

1. **Watching TV:** yes, this includes Netflix, Hulu, and whatever else you want to call it: passively staring into a glowing screen.
2. **Social media:** unless you're on a Facebook fast, this should be an easy one to drop or at least take 30 minutes out of.
3. **Reading:** I know, I know, "Hey, the author is saying we can toss reading out the window!" But if you read a ton, maybe you take half an hour to write instead of read.
4. **Alcohol:** if I don't drink a drop of alcohol in the evening, I wake up at least half an hour earlier the next morning.
5. **Fasting:** if you eat less after, say, 4 pm, your body has less work to do at night while you're sleeping and you sleep deeper and need less of it (i.e. I always wake up earlier and more refreshed when I skip dinner the night before).

There's a quick 5. Find something in there? Maybe you have something else that would be easy (or hard!) to remove? Great.

- **Possible:** add (cram even more into your day)
- **Impossible:** add (without removing and thinking it's all going to fit)
- **Repossible:** via negativa (remove something to provide room to add)

In true Create form, I just wrote this chapter immediately after I received a link from my pal Rich Robinson.

It was an article about Via Negativa and it came in at just the right time as I work on this book.

I had a choice to make.

1. I could have written him a long note back.
2. I could have read the article and done nothing with it.
3. I could have not read the article.

Yet, I chose to skip those 3 and Create something that was directly applicable to what I was working on: this chapter.

## 8

# WHEN IS THE ABSOLUTE PERFECT TIME TO START YOUR MASTERPIECE?

### HINT: IT'S NOT NEXT THURSDAY

"The best time to plant a tree was 20 years ago. The second best time is now."

— CHINESE PROVERB

When the tea is hot, the sun just ascended the horizon, your pen is full of ink and ...
Yeah, that's not going to happen.
Here's when, exactly, to get started with that dream project. I managed to:

1. Move the sunset,
2. Arrange the sand dunes,
3. Get the birds to sing on cue,
4. Stop time.

OK, fine, I didn't get any of that done.
In fact, I have it all here in poor lighting, out-of-focus, not-exactly-scripted 4 minutes of create-masterpiece.repossible.com.

Maybe you could wait for the frothy chai latte. That we could wait for.

Otherwise, it's time to get rolling.

- **Possible:** wait longer
- **Impossible:** time travel
- **Repossible:** plant the tree today

# PART III

# REPEAT

"We are what we repeatedly do. Excellence, then, is not an act, but a habit."

— Will Durant

## 9

# THE HABIT IS THE GOAL
PRACTICE IS PERFECT

"The obstacle is the way."

— Ryan Holiday

What if the goal were not to write a bestseller but to write every single day?
*...and become a writer in the meantime.*

Not to run a marathon but to jog every day ... *and get in shape while at it.*

Not to lose 10 pounds but to drink a liter more of water every day *...and clean and rejuvenate the body in doing so.*

What if practice didn't make perfect but **practice is perfect**?

**What if the goal were the daily habit?**

We're here in Create. I'm suggesting you create. Yet you may be thinking:

"What mountain-size monstrosity am I supposed to be creating?"

— You. Maybe.

This is where the good news comes in.

> *Speaking of which, this book is full of good news. It's not a book about how we shouldn't eat sugar or learning tax accounting for small- and medium-sized businesses.*

We're here talking about a **tiny daily action** that may—or may not—lead to some delicious result.

Got 4 minutes? Have a look at create-practice.repossible.com and let's relish in the idea that **our goal is tiny**. Our dream, our desired outcome, our measuring stick, is something so small and seemingly insignificant that after a while we forget we're doing it.

- **Possible:** goal
- **Impossible:** goal is goal
- **Repossible:** habit

If you still have a mountain in front of you (and not a molehill), here's a dorky thing to do but dorky things often work.

Repeat to yourself. Whispering it usually helps. Just these words:

"My goal is tiny. My goal is tiny. My goal is tiny."

— You (in a whisper)

## 10

# **OFFENSE & DEFENSE**
## GO FORTH, LOOK AHEAD, AND CREATE

"I am a slow walker, but I never walk back."

— Abraham Lincoln

*A*ction or reaction? Cause or effect? Create or consume? Tim Ferriss was talking with Derek Sivers and talking about offense and defense.

It was one of those moments when "my" idea was explained through someone else's words and it:

1. Hammered it home for me.
2. Gave me another way to explain it.
3. Deepened my understanding of where I'm going with it.

With Create, I want people to express, let it out, set it free, make, do, create.

To create is to go on offense, to go on the offensive.

It's going on offense before you need the defense. In fact, maybe **if you're on offense, you don't need the defense**, or at least need less of it.

It's a choice. It's up to you what side you want to play.

Or at least how much of which side.

Of course, you could also choose to not play the game at all and sit on the sidelines but you are someone who is deep into a book called Create so you're just not the type to sit on the sidelines.

I see this in people who say they're *bored*. I don't really believe in bored. If you have a body, a pulse, a brain, that all function—even a little bit—then you can create, you can go on offense.

Then all of the noise out there, what the world is going on and on about, the troubles and challenges of others, seem less important, less of a problem because you're on offense, you're creating.

You're more powerful.

You're *busy with stuff*.

You're on offense.

You're becoming more you.

You're you.

- **Possible:** defense
- **Impossible:** sidelines
- **Repossible:** offense

# 5-WORD HOOKS AND CONSTRAINT BREEDS CREATIVITY

### NOT 4, NOT 6. 5.

> "Vigorous writing is concise. A sentence should contain no unnecessary words, a paragraph no unnecessary sentences, for the same reason that a drawing should have no unnecessary lines and a machine no unnecessary parts."
>
> — WILLIAM STRUNK, JR.

Author Brian Meeks has an exercise for your book titles in which he suggests you come up with a bunch of 5-word hooks for the book.

He's flexible on the number, could be 4 or 6 or whatever.

I'm less flexible.

I like 5.

**Constraint Breeds Creativity**

You're reading a book. It's a collection of ideas, actions, information.

Doing the 5-word hook exercise, I can work with a limited number of words to try to convey the message I want to get across.

I won't pretend it's easy. It's tough.
Here's a short list I did for this book.

1. Turn off the screen. Create.
2. Step away from the screen.
3. You can consume. But create.
4. I measure happiness by creation.
5. What have you created lately?
6. Spill your secret power
7. Unleash what you bottled up
8. Unlock your secret creativity
9. What I Create Is Me
10. I Am What I Create
11. I Knew I Had It
12. Had I Only Looked Deeper
13. Consuming is easy. Try creating.
14. Need a burst of energy?
15. Seeking magical energy? Create something.
16. Seeking magical energy? Create some.
17. Release your secret super power

But I'd like to take it step further.

**Brand New U.**

The exercise is powerful because although you feel constrained by the number of words, it gets your brain working in a different way.

Your brain wants to find an answer. It becomes a game. Almost like when you're in Vegas and you have the terrible idea to "make up for the money I've lost by betting even bigger" but in this case, it's just five words and you're not going to spend your son's college money.

I'm going to go out on a limb here, go crazy for a minute, and suggest we do an exercise of just 5 words as a tagline not for your book, not for your company or service but for **you**.

Yep, you. The person.

5 words.
Ideally a phrase, not just 5 keywords.

I'm going to do it right now. I promise I'll do 5 of them and won't edit.

I should record this on video.

Ooh, wait, I will.

**5-Word Hooks for Bradley**

1. Who will you be next? (OK, that's cheating, that's the tagline for Repossible—but I feel it's really for me.)
2. Better together is for me
3. I am what I create
4. I create what I am
5. Who will I be next?
6. This is going pretty well (yes, a commentary on what I'm doing but also a meta observation on how I do things—do it, we'll see)
7. Author, Speaker, Teacher, We'll See
8. Here's my hand. Come up.
9. This is me helping you.
10. There is always more love.

*Ha! I just recorded it. You can find it at create-hooks.repossible.com. Search for 5-Word Hooks.*

I LOVE this exercise. It's so hard, it's deep, it can be painful, but it's usually extremely helpful and telling.

I think we're done here.

Oh wait.

Did you do yours?

Up for sharing? I'll make it possible to share yours at create-hooks.repossible.com.

- **Possible:** do 4 words—or 6
- **Impossible:** think about it some more
- **Repossible:** 5 words, Brand New U., right now

## 12

# TRIGGER DAILY CLARITY
### EVERY TIME I WALK INTO THE WOODS…

"An unfortunate thing about this world is that the good habits are much easier to give up than the bad ones."

— W. Somerset Maugham

To create new habits, it's easiest if we create a ritual or a trigger to know we're going to get started.

Every time I walk into the woods:

1. My mind becomes more clear
2. My ideas grow bolder
3. My fears spill into the ground
4. My dreams soar among the trees
5. The birds tell me what to do next

That's just a few steps into the woods.

My dad used to have a piece of chocolate after dinner. He really enjoyed it. In fact, it got to the point where if we didn't have any chocolate in the house and dinner was over, he would get antsy.

Dinner meant it was almost chocolate time.

Yep, the "bad" ones are harder to kick than new (good!) ones are to create.

Still, find the trigger, create a ritual, go a little nutty with it.

Watch professional athletes and their rituals. Each time that Steph Curry makes a 3-pointer, he taps his chest and points upwards. It's his ritual or even prayer or thank you for making the shot.

Yet, we can do the same before something happens.

I walk into the forest.

What do you do?

What could you do?

Where might be your "creative space" where you'll let your ideas arrive without having to go through security or customs?

Let's make up a simple one just for example's sake here. Say you want just a bit of clarity in your life. It could be for anything, short-term decisions such as what to make for dinner all the way to some help with your next career choice.

Create a daily ritual, a physical symbol, a motion, even a whispered mantra to let you know, "Hey, here we go. It's about to get real around here." Then give yourself the time to do the thing.

It could be as simple and quick as:

1. Brushing your teeth with your eyes closed and letting the humming brush shake loose your **next fabulous idea.** Twice a day. Boom.
2. Taking just two tiny little extra minutes after your shower to sit down, in the bathroom, on the toilet if there's nowhere else (PRO TIP: close the lid first), and with some deep and slow breathing, **shed the dread** of your upcoming day and gather the strength to go on the offensive. (Ooh, "shed the dread," I like that! See, I'm "being creative" here sharing tips on how to let creativity in!)
3. While on a walk, even if it's a short as around the block or to the mailbox, take out the earbuds, put your phone in your pocket, and just listen. What do you hear? Birds?

Cars? Dogs? **Filter everything else out** and hear what you want to focus on.

There you have it, 3 extremely non-scientific but possibly powerful triggers to get you started to tap into your deeper knowledge, your quick-witted charm, and a bit of the unknown.

Relish it. Do it daily. Follow the trigger.

- **Possible:** wait for perfection to arrive magically
- **Impossible:** change yesterday's trigger
- **Repossible:** trigger daily clarity

# PART IV

# EDUCATE

"Creative activity could be described as a type of learning process where teacher and pupil are located in the same individual."

— Arthur Koestler

## 13

# WHAT IF YOUR INPUT IS NETFLIX AND INSTAGRAM?
## WHAT ARE YOU POSSIBLY GOING TO OUTPUT? TO CREATE?

"All my friends are like, 'Can you be on my side in the zombie apocalypse?' and I'm like, 'I got this.'"

— Taissa Farmiga

So, uh, yeah, this: What if your input is Netflix and Instagram? What are you possibly going to output? To create?

Oh, and you're a 15-year-old boy.

Sure, there's school. But other than that.

What's your "output" going to be? Conversations, monologues with yourself. What do you write, say, do, tell, spell out for people?

What do you know? What do you love? What do you want to be?

Am I missing something? I usually am, so it wouldn't be a first.

Just trying to see things from that other perspective.

You know the one.

The one that's not your own.

- **Possible:** zombie
- **Impossible:** creator

- **Repossible:** zombie creator

In case that wasn't clear and I was being overly secretive about 15-year-old boys and their habits (I live with two teenage boys...enough said), here's how it's going to be when you come to let it out, when you finally decide to shed the mask, and create.

It's going to be, wait, I sense a numbered list coming...

1. Difficult
2. Painful
3. Slow
4. Yucky
5. Ouch
6. Can I stop now? This hurts.
7. Nasty
8. What's the opposite of confidence building?
9. Empty
10. Soul sucking

OK, I'll stop.
That hurt. Let's move on.

## 14

# GIVE THE GIFT OF YOU
### IF YOU HAVE NOTHING ELSE TO OFFER, YOU AT LEAST CAN GIVE YOUR ATTENTION

"The best way to cheer yourself up is to try to cheer somebody else up."

— Mark Twain

What gift can you give others? I guess you could give them an ice cream. Or you could do this.

I've spent the past few days helping my nieces record their books as narrators for the audiobook version.

We're done.

I'm still editing.

But I gave them something only I could give:

- my time
- my attention
- my experience
- my enthusiasm
- my confidence.

I listened to them, I guided them, I was there for them.

So simple.

What do you have to offer?

Give it to them.

Let's just change the ownership from the list above and now turn it into yours. Ready, here it comes.

**What You Can Give**

- your time
- your attention
- your experience
- your enthusiasm
- your confidence.

You have it. Maybe they don't. For at least one of these, you have more than they do. Find that one. Give that.

In the video below, I'm on the bridge but I'm not jumping off—although I'm way over to the side—over at create-gift.repossible.com.

- **Possible:** get
- **Impossible:** give without getting
- **Repossible:** give

## 15

# HOW YOU MAKE THEM FEEL
WHAT IF YOU THOUGHT ABOUT THIS EARLIER THAN LATER?

"I've learned that people will forget what you said, people will forget what you did, but people will never forget how you made them feel."

— Maya Angelou

Maybe it's the mathematician in me who wants to deconstruct things and put things into formulas and make systems.

Because if Maya Angelou says it's really about "how they're going to feel" then can't we create our content with that in mind?

"When you know what you want your reader to feel, you can write your book more easily."

— Bradley Charbonneau

It's not what you give or what they take or learn.

When they look back and think of you, it's the only thing that they'll remember: how you made them feel.

Here we are early in the creative process. In your book (or article or product or song or painting), when your reader/buyer/client finishes your book (etc.), how do they feel?

OK, sure, it's tough to predict the future.

So how would you like them to feel? What would be the ideal? **Write that down.**

> **PRO TIP:** *Use the form of a* **quote** *or a* **review** *or a* **blurb**. *What that reader might say or write after they finished your work.*

Let's do a meta exercise right here and how. Here we are in Create. We're, I don't know exactly, half way through? How do you feel?

How do I, as the author, hope that you, the reader, feels?

I'll take a stab but I'm also going to "aim high" and go for the feelings I hope you have (or will have) with this book and bonus content.

> "I read Create and I was motivated, sure. But when I actually started creating something, you know, truly making something, that's when the fireworks started."
>
> "It turns out, I'm a creator! I just didn't know it. This book gave me permission to call what I was already doing "creating" and now I feel stronger, more powerful, confident, and happy."
>
> "I often told people, "I'm just not a creative person." But it turns out, Mr. Charbonneau's book "Create" isn't really about being creative, it's about creating and making and getting it done. Now I call myself a creator. Well, not to the public. At least not yet."
>
> "OMG. I'm a creator! Who knew?"
>
> "It was that chapter called "How you make them feel" which turned things around for me. I did those quotes he asked us to do and then I knew what I had to write. The process was counter intuitive, but it worked."

I just cranked those out fairly painlessly. It's because I'm deep in "creation" mode writing this book. When you're working on something, sorry, playing with something, you feel it more, quotes like this come more naturally, and it's, wait for it, wait for it, it's more fun.

Come on over to create-feel.repossible.com for a more 3D feel for this topic.

- **Possible:** create
- **Impossible:** know what they feel beforehand
- **Repossible:** forecast what you'd like them to feel

## 16

# JUST STOP (FOR THE DAY)
### LET GO OF THE DAY

> "We all have a personal recipe for productivity. One person may need six cups of autonomy and just a pinch of collaboration. Another person may require heaps of sociability and noise, with just a teaspoon of occasional privacy."
>
> — NEIL BLUMENTHAL

Morning person? Great. Know when to call it a day.

For me, it's about 3 pm.

On "smart" days, I will just stop. I won't even try anymore--at least not for anything creative.

I know (the creative part of) the day is gone.

Sure, I can push it, I can force it. I might get a little goodness. But it's going to be 80/20.

Get to sleep earlier, get started earlier tomorrow.

Enjoy the rest of day.

Let go of the day.

In my view—and that's just it, my view—the morning is for accomplishing and anything after the morning is to start "claiming accomplishments" so might as well call it quits around 3.

What works for you? Morning person? Night owl?

It doesn't matter which one as long as you know it and adhere to it.

- **Possible:** start
- **Impossible:** keep going
- **Repossible:** know when to stop—and do it

# 17

## CREATING CREATES MORE CREATIVITY ... EVEN WHILE DRIVING A CAR
### CREATING IS CONTAGIOUS

"The secret of getting ahead is getting started."

— MARK TWAIN

**B**ecause we cannot not create
As I write this, or rather, dictate this, I'm on highway A30 in the center of Holland. As of this writing, I don't know if dictating while driving is illegal yet but I'm doing it now while I still can.

Whenever I'm busy with a book (this is a bit of an inside joke because I am always busy with a book), it makes me think more deeply about topics the have any direct or indirect connection with what I'm working on.

10 minutes ago, I was listening to Seth Godin's latest book, "This is Marketing." He said something that changed my perspective. He said, "People like us do things like this."

Now you might be thinking this is very exclusionary, that it excludes certain groups and turns the dialogue into an "us versus them." However, as I listen further to Seth's insightful commentary, I realize he is talking about the **smallest viable audience** and how to connect with your readers or your fans or your clients or your customers.

> Just while driving, I stopped the audiobook and then, you'll be thankful to hear, I used audio commands to then open the voice recorder and dictate for the next 10 minutes how what I just heard was relevant to what I'm working on.

Each part of why I'm writing (or rather, dictating) this today is because:

**I don't have a lot of patience for people who say they don't have time to create.**

As I probably previously mentioned, I'm still driving in the car.

> [Editor's note: I came back later to copy and paste the transcript as well as add some formatting.]

It's not that I have a seven-hour journey in front of me and I figured I could get a little bit done or even that I thought I could get a whole lot done. No, I have another 10 minutes of my trip but, and yes, I'm going to quote myself here:

> "Creating is so important to me and gives me such pleasure enjoy and satisfaction and I will turn my Monday morning commute into a creation section where I bang out two chapters for two different books while driving in 130 km/h through the autumn golds in the middle of the Netherlands."
>
> — BRADLEY CHARBONNEAU

Yes, I just quoted myself. Why? Because I want to be known—if only to myself—as the guy who makes the time to create, he doesn't wait around for lightning to strike. **He is the lightning.**

Another reason I want to get this out and that I couldn't wait to pull over later is that creating creates more creation.

**Creating creates more creativity**

I have long given up any belief of the idea of writer's block. I have a much less well-known condition and that is an *addiction to creating*. Either way, it's also the antidote when I'm working on something.

I find more things relevant to what I'm working on than if I worked on that something. To put it another way:

**if I were working on nothing then I would find nothing relevant to relate to nothing.**

But when you're creating something, it's **infectious** and, creating one thing leads to creating another thing which usually creates many more things.

If I can write a chapter of a book while at this very moment at the offramp to my destination, then you might be able to understand a little bit more easily why I don't believe in a writer's block, excuses, and whining about how difficult it all is.

> *[Editor's note: I did get to my destination safe and sound and guess what? Now I have two chapters of two upcoming books. What are you doing during your commute?]*

- **Possible:** wait until you get home
- **Impossible:** lunar eclipses are the only time to create
- **Repossible:** hit record on your phone right now

# PART V
# AMPLIFY

"Money and success don't change people; they merely amplify what is already there."

— Will Smith

## 18

# LACKING CREATIVITY? TUNE INTO YOUR RADIO FREQUENCY.

### WHAT'S YOUR NUMBER?

"We cannot solve our problems with the same thinking we used when we created them."

— Albert Einstein

What if our brains could tune into the *right* frequency? Like a radio dial.

For those of you who don't remember what a *radio dial* is, I'll explain.

Before digital numbers on the radio, you used to have a round dial. You couldn't see any numbers for the stations (e.g. 98.3) so you had to fiddle with it, turn it back and forth, listen a little, and finally, maybe, you got a clear signal.

Maybe after a few seconds, you might adjust it again.

But usually, you could find a strong signal and you'd get a clear connection.

This is how I see creativity.

Without going too much off the deep end (well, at least not yet, but I will for sure), I see us as radios that "tune in" to frequencies.

Once we can connect, we're clear and we can leave the dial intact and we're good to go.

When we're connected, when the dial is in the right place, we feel right, we're clever, quick, and have answers. We can make decisions easily, we answer questions with authority and little to no doubt, we are proud.

It's a delightful place to be.

A few years ago, I was pretty sure to create anything, to make something, to succeed, you had to:

1. Struggle
2. Wait
3. Fail
4. Try some more
5. Give up
6. Get back on the horse
7. Pout
8. Stick with it
9. Forget it
10. Ugh

That's how it used to go. That was before I knew **why I was supposed to create.** I thought it was for:

1. Me
2. Success
3. Money
4. Pride
5. Lamborghinis

OK, I didn't really think it was for #5.

Now I know why to create. I create because:

1. I can't not do it
2. It's like oxygen (it's hard to survive, much less thrive,

without it)
3. It's how I surpass wherever I was
4. It's how to get ahead of where I am
5. It's the only way to see beyond where I think I might be

Whew. Heavy stuff, right? Serious. Big time. Whoa. Scary.
Not at all.
Remember the radio dial? It's as simple as that. We need to connect, to find our frequency. Once we're there, remove hand from dial and let it flow.
Sound easy? It is.
Did you catch the part where I said I figured out **why** I create? That helps.
It's really #3 above: to "surpass wherever I was." To get better, to learn, to find purpose and meaning.
I hear you whispering...

"Bradley, the whole radio dial thing is great and all, but **how** do I find my frequency?"

— You (whispering)

Do you play tennis? Golf? Baseball?
When you connect with the ball in just the right spot, it takes less power, less energy from you and the ball goes even further.
Pretty cool, right:

1. Less energy
2. Better results

This is the radio dial. When it's right on the number, when the connection is good, it's clear.
For you, when it feels right, when there's little or no static, when you're in a flow state, when it comes easily, when time flies, then you're on the right frequency, then you know you're

connected to a higher sense of self and what you're doing is working.

- **Possible:** live with the static
- **Impossible:** go digital
- **Repossible:** find your frequency

## 19

## **CREATING IS FUN!**
### BUT I CAN'T CONVINCE YOU

"The emotional power of creating something... Nothing gives me as much joy as that."

— Sigrid

There's a chapter in this book called "Cre8." I left it in even though it's more just "some ideas about a possible project" and not a perfectly-penned chapter.

In that chapter, I write:

"I'm having fun just creating this thing."

— Me, in the chapter titled "Cre8"

Now, I suppose "fun" is subjective. Something I consider fun might not be something you think is fun.

I'm going to go out on a limb and declare that creating is (or should be or at least could be) for everyone.

I think of the author and the blank page. When you don't know what to say, it's a threatening piece of landscape.

But when the pen starts flowing—or you force it to start—it can lead to discovery, the unknown, and joy.

But just like I can't tell you what an avocado tastes like, I can't tell you that creating is fun.

You're going to have to get there on your own.

Let me whisper it to ask you to make your way there: there are few joys as powerful and as delightful and as fun as creating.

- **Possible:** do it
- **Impossible:** don't do it
- **Repossible:** allow the joy in doing it

## 20
## "I HAVE NOTHING TO OFFER."
### I DON'T BELIEVE YOU

"If you hold a cat by the tail you learn things you cannot learn any other way."

— Mark Twain

Someone told me the other night that she had nothing to offer.

I didn't believe her.

Not that she was lying but maybe she just didn't know.

But I've been there. I used think I didn't have anything to offer. Now I can't hold back everything I have to offer.

What happened?

I started making, doing, giving, getting it out there. Getting it out of you.

In recent years, I "find what I have to offer" by putting my phone into its little grip tripod, attaching it to a tree branch and hitting record.

Find the 5-minute "I have nothing to offer" video at create-nothing.repossible.com.

There's a chapter in this book about a radio dial. I see the idea of

"I have nothing to offer" in the same light as the radio dial in that you might think you have nothing to offer but it's more a case that you might just not know who is seeking what you are offering.

In radio dial terms, if you're broadcasting at 89.7 megahertz and your audience (be it your boss, your family or your cat) is receiving only signals below 85.3 megahertz then no, you don't have anything to offer them at that time on that frequency.

Radio dial imagery not working on you?

If a dentist talks technical shop to a group of ballerinas, they're not going to get him. He might say, "I have nothing to offer." and, well, he'd be right that he has nothing to offer them in that situation with that message.

So nope, I don't believe people who say:

I have nothing to offer.

It's more a question of what are you offering to whom, when, and why.

Tune that dial. Check your frequency. Know theirs frequency.

Because you do have something to offer and your audience is out there seeking it.

- **Possible:** something to offer
- **Impossible:** nothing to offer
- **Repossible:** match your frequency (with your audience)

## 21

## YOU ARE NOT ALONE
### EVEN IF IT FEELS LIKE YOU ARE

"If you knew who walked beside you at all times, on the path that you have chosen, you could never experience fear or doubt again."

— Wayne Dyer

Well, even if you think you're alone, you're not alone. A third party, a different perspective, a partner, a collaborator, even just a sounding board. But someone who isn't you.

I went it alone for years. And years. Then more of those. It's probably decades.

There is probably a type of insect in the savanna of Botswana that lives out its entire existence in solitary—and it's all good.

But we're human.

We want to collaborate, work together, uh, I mean, play together.

We're better together. If I can write books together with my 17-year-old nieces then anybody can pretty much collaborate with anyone. Here's proof: create-together.repossible.com.

- **Possible:** compete

- **Impossible:** close (your eyes)
- **Repossible:** collaborate

## 22

# FEELING STUCK? BOGGED DOWN? POP THAT BOIL, LET IT OUT, CREATE.
## POPCORN KERNEL SHELL IN YOUR TEETH

"It's not the size of the dog in the fight, it's the size of the fight in the dog."

— MARK TWAIN

Sorry about the boil imagery there in the title, but can you feel it?

That's how creativity gets stuck inside of us.

Or rather, dare I go out on a limb to say, how "stuff" gets stuck in us and how letting it out is key.

We consume. Lots. No, like way tons all the time. We watch, we listen, we read. It's all coming in.

**Where and when and how do we let it out?**

I am nowhere near a medical doctor, but I like the boil (or the cyst or pimple or zit) metaphor.

It's this nasty thing that's going to hurt a little to pop, but the relief we'll feel when it's open is worth it.

So worth it.

You know the feeling. Let's see if I can bring it home for you with other bodily yuck:

1. **Stuck in your teeth:** for me, it's usually those little shells around the popcorn kernel. When I get that out from the deep crevice between my tooth and gum, I'm ready to donate my life savings to charity in gratitude. It's that much relief.
2. **Splinters:** wasn't it a little <u>mouse who removed the splinters from the lion</u>? Although the lion is (was!) mighty and the king of the jungle, a little thorn was killing him. Relieving his pain, done by a tiny mouse, set him free.
3. **Vomit party:** OK, I completely realize I'm deep in the gross-out mode but it's working. You ate and/or drank the wrong something. It's not sitting right. You could wait it out. Or your body doesn't wait. It wants it out of you. Now. Blech! Vloooom! Blaaaaah! Nasty, icky, but out of you and gone and you're a new person.

Our thoughts and ideas and creativity and imagination work in much the same fashion. If we just keep cramming it all in, it's going to get full, overloaded, even sick.

At some point, you're going to have to let it go.

We can let it out on a regular basis, or we can wait until we're ready to, yeah, sorry, puke our guts out.

### My Non-Medical Cure

Let it out. Set it free. A little bit on a regular basis. How often? Daily seems to be the best schedule. Why? Because it's easy to remember.

Did you know that prescriptions that are prescribed as "bi-weekly" or even "every other day" get forgotten? Why? Because we can't remember when we last took it.

With the daily **Pimple Popping Party**, it's easy: it's today. Here's a quick test:

1. Have you popped your creative pimple today? (Yes / No)
2. Yes? Great! You're all set. Done for the day. Woo hoo! Celebration time.

3. No? Get it done. When? Now is good. But before 11:59 PM.

**How or What to Create**
I hear you. I hear many of you whispering:

"But Bradley, I don't know how or what to create! How can I prevent my enormous white-tipped zit from exploding into my chai latte?"

— You

I'm a writer. For me, it's easy: just start writing. On a napkin with a pen borrowed from the waitress. Typing into a laptop. Even dictating to Siri.

Just a little. Just until it's out. Might be 5 minutes. Might be 50 minutes. Doesn't matter. You'll feel it. Like when you're ready to wipe your mouth off of spittle. You just know.

If writing isn't your thing, how else can you let it out? Let us count the ways.

1. **Dictate:** speak it into your phone. I bet your phone has a recording app built in. Pretend it's a letter to your late grandmother (who you loved, right?). Or talk to your future daughter. Let her know what's stuck inside of you right now. Take 2 minutes. Might be all you need.
2. **Move:** run, walk, hike, go up (and down) the stairs. Don't listen to a podcast, don't think about work. Focus on your legs moving, your feet one in front of the other. Talk to yourself. Out loud if there's no one around and/or if you're comfortable with it. Get out of breath at least a little so you have to focus on your breathing (you know, to stay alive and all). Then what's your next thought? Focus on that one. Got it? Good, done for the day.
3. **Draw:** I'm a terrible drawer. See, I bet drawer isn't even a word. No, it's a word, it's a thing you put socks into. (Focus!) If you're at the stick figure level or you can paint a

gorgeous landscape, put pencil to paper and doodle your thoughts. What does it look like in your brain? What wants to get out? Pen, paper, go.

What do you do to let it out? We take so much in, how do we let it out? What works for you?

- **Possible:** pretend you're fine
- **Impossible:** hold it in
- **Repossible:** barf onto the page

## 23

# ARE YOU WORKING ON ANOTHER BOOK?

### IF I'M NOT, I'M…

"I don't know, but I probably am."

— Arthur Miller

The above is the answer given to Dr. Wayne Dyer when asking playwright Arthur Miller, "Are you working on another play?"

**I no longer know what it's like to not be working on another book.**

*And I hope I never know that feeling.*

Arthur Miller was 88-years old when he answered that question. He died the next year.

Where is the source that provides him with what he writes? What is the foundation from which it spouts?

"You just have to surrender and say thank you."

— Dr. Wayne Dyer

Of course I'm working on another book. I'm working on several books all the time. I think the only time I won't be working on another book is when I take my last breath, but maybe that last breath will be one more idea. Maybe that last idea I take with me into the next life (whatever that may be) and I will start again.

I no longer know how not to create, to produce, to make and make believe and it's what keeps me going day in and day out.

It's creating, it's building, it's part of, I don't know of another word: a legacy.

But it's not because I want to leave something behind. It's that it's my way forward. I write to live. I write not only to survive, but to thrive.

Am I working on another book? I have so many answers:

- Of course.
- Is there another state of mind?
- Yes.
- Aren't we all?
- Aren't you?

Speaking of which, I got to get back to some Charlie Holiday.

- **Possible:** start
- **Impossible:** finish
- **Repossible:** play

# PART VI

# TRUST

"The more you trust your intuition, the more empowered you become, the stronger you become, and the happier you become."

— Gisele Bundchen

# 24

# OH NO, NOT THE APOCALYPSE!
## IT'S THE END OF THE WORLD! BUT IS IT THE END OF YOUR WORLD?

"The mark of your ignorance is the depth of your belief in injustice and tragedy. What the caterpillar calls the end of the world, the Master calls the butterfly."

— RICHARD BACH

*A* dear friend of mine (who I honest and truly love) often sends me (really long) articles about, oh, I don't know, the apocalypse and other light reading.

Let me summarize one of them in bullet points (because we all know the entire universe can be summarized in bullet points and "5-Word Hooks," right?).

## Apocalyptic Highlights for Giggles

1. agenda of totalitarian control
2. frightened public accepts abridgments of civil liberties
3. destruction of small business

4. irrational rejection of information that might disrupt normalcy and comfort
5. civilization's established institutions are increasingly helpless
6. establishing the state's sovereignty over our bodies
7. epidemic is some monstrous plot perpetrated by evildoers

I'm maybe halfway through the article and I already got these goodies above. I bet you can't wait to read it, too!

For the sake of argument, let's say the apocalypse is here, the world is ending, and, oh, whatever, the government has hijacked our minds and ... OK, OK, you get the idea.

So you're on your deathbed and you're thinking back over your life and I can almost guarantee that none of the 7 items listed above are going to be what you talk about with your kids at your bedside—at least I don't wish that upon you as your final thoughts.

So what ARE you going to be talking about?

**What you created in your life.**

OK, yes, I'm completely biased. Here we are in a book titled Create, of course, I'm all in favor of creating over "irrational rejection of information that might disrupt normalcy and comfort" but partly because I'm not even sure what that sentence means.

Maybe I'm just not intelligent enough to understand the articles my well-meaning friend sends me.

But you know what I'd rather receive from him?

Something **he created.**

If he drew a picture, even a stick figure, maybe wrote his own article, recorded a voice message, stood in front of his phone and sent me a video report of how fast the grass is growing, it would be more "meaningful" to me because it came from him, directly from him, maybe influenced by the long essays he reads, but at least it's *his* message, *his* voice, *his* creation.

You know why I don't care about the apocalypse? Because it's the external world coming towards me.

Even if the entire planet is scorched and there's nothing left, I am that seedling that's sprouting from the rubble.

*I have no fear because I am creating.*

I'm the tiny insect who survived the end of the world who's going to stretch its little limbs, look around, and see what he can create (or find to eat).

I absolutely acknowledge I'm simplifying what is probably a complex scenario.

But is it?

**I create therefore I am.**

In the apocalypse, I have my creation. I'm creating my own world, my own environment, so it's not "affected" by external forces. It can't be because it's inside of me. Yes, I let it out, but the roots are deep within me and they are mine.

I'm creating my own world.

Apocalypse schmalocalypse.

- **Possible:** global apocalypse
- **Impossible:** internal apocalypse
- **Repossible:** seedling

## 25

# THERE ARE NO GAZELLES IN THERAPY
## LION? WHAT LION?

"It's not stress that kills us, it is our reaction to it."

— Hans Selye

The lion attacks, the gazelles run, they escape--or not! A few minutes later, they're back to eating grass and chatting about the blue sky.

I'm not as fast as they are but because I create every day, the external "threats" and fears and dangers of the world concern me less--and if they do, it's temporary.

My drive, my energy, my power comes from within and nothing can dim that light.

I'm outdoors, no lions in sight right here at create-gazelles.repossible.com.

- **Possible:** stress
- **Impossible:** avoid stress
- **Repossible:** get over it

## 26

# FROM "WHY ME?" TO "WHY NOT ME?"
### A FIRST-TIME AUTHOR WALKS INTO A BOOKSTORE…

"If you're early on in your career and they give you a choice between a great mentor or higher pay, take the mentor every time. It's not even close. And don't even think about leaving that mentor until your learning curve peaks."

— STANLEY DRUCKENMILLE

The power of a mentor.
    Alone, we can only get so far. We walk into the bookstore for the first time as a budding author and we're probably intimidated.

A mentor can help.

They have something we don't (at least in an ideal mentee-mentor relationship): experience.

It's a simple, three-step process from experience to exchange to mindset. If you reverse it and spell it out, it turns out, it's all about **me**. Well, not ME, but MEE.

*A first-time author walks into a bookstore…*

It's not a joke. It's more of a tragedy.
Or maybe it's a comedy.
Or maybe it's a documentary.
That first-time author, the novice, the beginner has one of two thoughts when she walks into the bookstore.
They both start with the same statement:

"Look at all of those books."

— Inexperienced Author

But then the question they ask is where the great divide sinks in:

1. How could I possibly compete with all of those authors?
2. If all of those guys can do it, why can't I?

It's All About **MEE** and it's a three-step process:

1. **M:** Mindset
2. **E:** Exchange
3. **E:** Experience

I'll walk through the steps complete with "live drawing" over at create-mee.repossible.com.

- **Possible:** why me?
- **Impossible:** skip experience
- **Repossible:** why not me?

## 27

# SHOOT OFF THE FLARE GUN OF YOUR PASSION AND SEE WHO TAKES NOTICE
## CO-CREATE

> "If you build it, they might come. But if you don't build it, they won't."
>
> — BRADLEY CHARBONNEAU

Who are good partners? Collaborators? Silent investors? We're not going to know if they don't know what we're doing.

As much as "we writers" want to hide out behind our typewriters (our what?) and Just Write, we need to send up the occasional flare to see who connects with us.

Let's go from:

1. "Wow, that's the stupidest idea of all time." to:
2. "You're a brilliant genius, let me help."

We're never going to know until we shoot up that flare gun of your passion: create-rocket.repossible.com.

- **Possible:** blow the dog whistle
- **Impossible:** mind readers
- **Repossible:** shoot off your flare gun of passion

## 28

# CRE8
### 8 DAYS TO CREATE

"Daring ideas are like chessmen moved forward; they may be beaten, but they may start a winning game."

— Johann Wolfgang von Goethe

We're here in the "Trust" section of this book. What you'll find below is a bit of stream of consciousness or notes about a possible project or product or service I saw related to Create.

I dare put it in here because we're in the section called "Trust" and it's not that I trust my ideas are so brilliant but I trust that someone, maybe you, will read something below and say something like, and maybe just to yourself:

"I'm glad he left this in here. I liked it. Especially _____."

— Maybe You

This is my level of trust to myself but also to you. I'm going out on a limb here and sharing something that was just a thought, maybe it's silly, maybe it's The Big Idea, I don't know.

My point is to trust ourselves, our ideas, and to share them because you never know what might happen if we create.

I have to add here that I even comment below, in writing, that I'm having fun putting this idea together, in working in out.

Although I just give it a slight mention here, it's one of the most important concepts in this book: **creating is fun.**

Here you have it, in its delicious raw form.

## A "course" (?) called Cre8

I see a variety of "media" to create. Not just writing and _____ (drawing, etc.) but, for example:

- Create | Focus
- Create | Clarity
- Create | Abundance
- Create | Freedom
- Create | Peace
- Create | Habits
- Create | Happiness

Sound like fun?
Then and/or maybe verbs/actions:

- Create | Draw
- Create | Sing
- Create | Write
- Create | Photograph
- Create | Narrate
- Create | ???

*This is fun already.*

A few guidelines or parameters (again, this stuff just comes to me clearly so I have to write it down ... see how I'm walking the talk?).

### The Instruction / Guidance

The "instruction" (video, audio) each day, the lesson, the guidance, must be:

- Under 2 minutes

This is because my electric toothbrush also goes off after two minutes. This means:

- We **have the time** each morning (because we're brushing our teeth each morning **anyway**, aren't we?)
- It's quick
- It's easy
- It's simple

### The Instructor / Leader / Teacher

I'd love for this to not always be me.

What if a **famous audiobook narrator** gave you one tip to narrate a story? Maybe he shows you how to use pauses. Then your action, your creation, for the day is to narrate a short piece of work. Maybe that piece is offered to you, maybe you find something on your own.

- A **singer** gave you a secret tactic to bring out another voice you didn't know you had.
- An **artist** taught you something about color and you colored something quickly.
- An **illustrator** helped you with a drawing.
- A **fiction writer** had you begin a fantasy story.

- A **nonfiction writer** asked you for help to outline your new product or idea.
- A **copywriter** worked with you to get your idea clear and into 6 words.

*I'm having fun just creating this thing.*

**Output, Accountability, Public**

Again, maybe I'm so comfortable with this that I no longer care or it no longer bothers me but I'd love for each participant to post 8 days of their 8 creations on a, for example, free WordPress.com site (that they created the day before as prep).

- **Possible:** think about a thing
- **Impossible:** make it perfect
- **Repossible:** dare to leave a "raw" idea in your published book

# 29

## A 14-YEAR-OLD TEENAGER, A 20-MINUTE DRIVE. DO WE HAVE TIME TO CREATE?
### IF YOU GET THEM STARTED AND ENCOURAGE THEM

"Flatter me, and I may not believe you. Criticize me, and I may not like you. Ignore me, and I may not forgive you. Encourage me, and I will not forget you. Love me and I may be forced to love you."

— WILLIAM ARTHUR WARD

We didn't have a sound studio. No backup vocals. We didn't even have the manual to Garage Band.
We did have:

1. 20 minutes
2. A "need" (I needed intro music for my podcast—or maybe for the videos in the accompanying bonus content to this book!)
3. Encouragement

That was about it and it was all we needed.
Dear Reader,
I'm not sure I can explain here the unbridled joy I felt as we drove east on the A12 highway.

My son is not looking at his phone, lost in space watching, consuming, or listening to whatever.

He's making something, creating a little song, a tiny, maybe 30-second intro bit of music for my podcast.

He's trying, he's failing, I'm encouraging, he's getting better, he puts together a bit of a violin, then some cello, he looks for Gregorian chanting but can't find it, so settles on some piano.

He creates a little song.

While we're in the car.

On the way to the store.

This is all we need.

Encouragement.

A little nudge, a push, a pull, a reminder, some love.

It's Sunday morning in the woods and I tell it like I see it over at create-20minutes.repossible.com.

- **Possible:** wait
- **Impossible:** perfect
- **Repossible:** try

# PART VII

# EVOLVE

"What's dangerous is not to evolve."

— Jeff Bezos

## 30

# DO SOMETHING DARING, FIND TRIBE, WRITE BOOK.
### YOU DON'T NEED TO GO IT ALONE

"It's important to find your tribe. If you can find people you can share ideas with, people you're mutually stimulated by it helps you move forward."

— KARLA CROME

et's put that chapter title into a numbered list, shall we?

1. Do something daring.
2. Find tribe.
3. Write book.

It sure beats the old way I was doing it.
Which was:

1. Do something daring.
2. Write book.

See that vital step #2 I was missing?

The turning point for me was Spark, book #8 in the Repossible series (which I wrote way before books 1-7 for reasons I can explain...).

**With Spark, I interviewed many people to get *their stories* to add to *my story*.**

Through their stories, my own story became *stronger*.

Through their stories, my perspective on the topic *changed* and *grew*.

Through talking with them, I learned about other angles, ideas, and even new (gasp) book ideas.

Just what I needed!

No, it is just what I need.

Work together with others. You become better. They become better. They help you even more. You help them even more.

It's like the vicious circle—but the good kind.

Co-creating at its best.

- **Possible:** alone
- **Impossible:** alone in parallel with others going it alone
- **Repossible:** spark

Yep, I'm going to keep going down here.

I know, I know, I did my Possible, Impossible, Repossible, but this is for those who *keep reading*.

This chapter may not seem it, but it's super important.

This book, Create, is important, yep. Creating, making, doing, building, learning, creating more, growing, rising up, you get the idea, you've been with me along the journey through this book.

But Spark takes thing to the next level.

I see Create as usually very solitary. For me, it's early in the morning, building off of a meditation session, then boom, jumping into writing or recording or speaking or whatever it is that morning.

But Spark, co-creating, working together with others, creating together with other people, it just blows it out of the water (to use the technical term for it).

Do you ever have it on a phone call or maybe out for dinner and you're talking away, listening, back and forth, exchanging ideas, and there's a lull in the conversation.

Then something drops. Like lightning. Then the thunder arrives.

You (usually) both feel it. Something just happened. You feel it more than you can pinpoint or even put your finger on it.

You connected. Something you and the other person said or discovered or even created just landed in your lap, in your mind, maybe in your heart, and you *felt* it land there. Like thunder when it's close: you feel it in your bones.

That's co-creating.

I know we're still in the Create book and it's mostly about creating on your own and I acknowledge that but I get excited about the *bigger* stuff, the loftier goals, the exciting and tears-in-my-eyes-while-walking-in-the-woods stuff.

We need to create on our own. Yep. Absolutely. But keep it in the back of your mind as you practice, as you keep creating, that someday, with someone, you're going to create together.

It's going to be special.

It's going to be unique.

Lightning will strike.

Then the thunder will rumble your heart.

## "I MEASURE MY LIFE BY WHAT I CREATE."
### NOT HOW MUCH I CONSUME

"Writing is a form of therapy; sometimes I wonder how all those who do not write, compose or paint can manage to escape the madness, melancholia, the panic and fear which is inherent in a human situation."

— Graham Greene

*A*re you passively sitting at home consuming?
I was listening to Joanna Penn's 10-year anniversary podcast (10 years of her blog, 10 years of her podcast is early next year) while biking home through the woods this morning.

She's a writer, podcaster, speaker. She's a maker, a doer. She builds things, creates something from nothing. She's a creator.

My 22nd book came out last month and I am really excited about ... my 23rd book: Create. Maybe it'll be my 24th book as "Ask" or "Meditation for Creatives" might sneak in the production line first.

But **that's exactly my point**: I'm creating.

I love creating. I can't not create. Without creating, I don't know what I'd do with myself.

Sure, I love to sit in a movie theater as much as the next person. I treasure being taken away in a story between the pages of my favorite novels. But the gauge I use to test what you truly love is when, for example, you (accidentally?) get up early on a Sunday morning, no one else is awake, you have an hour or two of completely free, unexpected time to yourself and ... what do you choose to do?

I'll usually write.

If I'm feeling particularly whimsical, I'll write fiction.

Below are some quotes from Joanna from her podcast episode last week. I listened to them, backed up, and typed them out because they're just that important to me. If you'd like to listen to the full episode, you can find your favorite podcast link here: <u>From First Book To A Multi-Six-Figure Writing Business: 10 Years Of The Creative Penn</u>.

> "I've always felt that being an indie author as a movement but I think it's part of this bigger maker movement. People never believed that humans would want to do this. The big publishers probably thought that the most of us are just passively sitting at home consuming whereas actually people want to create."
>
> "You can see this shift in big brands to artisan products ... independent creators."
>
> "We are a self-sustaining ecosystem of authors. Everyone who writes a book buys more books than they will ever write."
>
> "If you're someone who believes that every author is your competitor, you're going to be unhappy."
>
>    "I measure my life by what I create."
>
> — JOANNA PENN

I should add that I feel particularly connected to Joanna as a fellow creator as we've shared a similar fateful past of being an ... SAP consultant! The horror!

Then we both came to our senses, turned a corner, and chose to lead the lives we were meant to live.

As *creators*.

Thank you, Joanna, for leading the way. This chapter is for you. I look forward to following in your footsteps as you thrive forward.

We're rooting for you to lead the way.

- **Possible:** follow
- **Impossible:** stop the creators
- **Repossible:** lead

## 32

# AFRAID IT ISN'T REAL
### IT'S ALMOST DREAMLIKE

"My happiness is so great that it makes me almost afraid."

— Theodore Roosevelt

*P*art of the process of writing books (and building out ideas and concepts) is to take someone else's perspective and analyze it, work with it, try to see it from their view, let it sink in, and then go further with your original idea.

I look for quotes from others to get that perspective on an idea.

Mr. Theodore Roosevelt up there would have slipped right by me had I not had the exact same feeling as he did: the happiness is so great, so deep, so pure that I sometimes have to look around or pinch myself to see if it's real.

I'm fully aware that there are chapters in this book you might not relate to or even believe. I get that.

Who am I to prance around and say I'm so happy creating that I don't even believe it sometimes?

But here I am saying just that.

I just want to whisper it in your ear that there are higher states to strive towards where we create and it makes us giddy, happy, full of life and meaning and purpose.

I know that's a bold statement.

It is there. It is possible. It will come.

- **Possible:** accept
- **Impossible:** deny
- **Repossible:** smile and wave, boys, smile and wave*

*From "Madagascar" film.

## 33

# TONY
### ONE OF MY HEROES

"Comme si, comme ça. Sometimes a little more si than ça."

— Tony

The above quote was how Tony often answered the question, "How are you?"

At 100+ years of age, he still had a sense of humor.

I might dare say that thanks to his sense of humor, he lived to be 105.

## Still Creating at 105

Tony played a big role in my "Every Single Day" book. His passion, perseverance, and patience pretty much gave me the three "P's" I was seeking to become the author I am today.

Yet here we are in book #23 and I'm not only still creating but I still feel like I'm just getting started, I'm full of energy, and wake up each day to create.

I'm **not even half** of Tony's age and realizing that he was creating until he was 105 fills me with such joy, energy and just plain giddy happiness that I wanted to thank him yet again in this book.

I believe he made it that long in part because he was creating. He was making. Painting, drawing, sculpting, using his imagination to make something out of nothing.

If you ever thought you were too old to start something or maybe you didn't have the creativity or the technology. Maybe you thought your diet wasn't right to begin (make note of Tony's diet in the video below).

Creating your way to a long, healthy, and happy life.

Could the secret be not just a positive outlook but an active imagination? Active meaning you use it, you create things from nothing.

I recorded this video not knowing that my dear friend Tony passed away today.

I hope you can take his 105-year existence and bring even a drop of joy into your life.

He creates something from nothing.

It's easy. I promise.

There's a tribute to Tony here: create-tony.repossible.com.

- **Possible:** create today
- **Impossible:** plan to create once you're 105
- **Repossible:** create now as if you're 105

## 34

# HOW TO GO FROM NOTHING TO EVERYTHING
## FROM NOTHING IS MAGICAL TO EVERYTHING IS MAGICAL

"If you're not in awe, you're not paying attention."

— Bumper Sticker

*I*t's both simple and easy.

I'm jet-lagged. Out of my rhythm. I'm tired, a zombie, my eyes are heavy. I'm not myself.

I'm in a place where <u>Nothing is Magical</u>. This may not seem like such a strange thing unless you're used to a state where <u>Everything is Magical</u>.

Now, I don't mean that I go around and see glitter in the leaves of the trees or a shimmer in the eyes of a person I pass by or that crystal-clear ideas come to me like snowflakes on a late-winter evening.

I couldn't possibly mean that I feel that my feet don't always touch the ground or I tend towards bringing out mostly only the good in people or my life seems like a circus event where tigers jump through the hoops of my memory and ignite the fiery flames of passion in the everyday.

And of course, I certainly wouldn't imply that I lead a charmed life where relationships with people are things I can see just like I can see someone's breath on a fresh fall morning.

I wouldn't dare suggest that I reside at a higher level, vibrate on a higher frequency, and somehow, manage to transform what might be seen as a regular human existence into a fairytale poem of fantasy.

I couldn't possibly mean all of that.

**Except that this is exactly what I mean.**

Precisely what I imply. Absolutely, completely, and precisely what I'm getting at.

Do you have to <u>descend</u> to <u>rise up</u>?

Yes.

Do you need to know where you came from to realize where you are?

Yes.

Do you need to live a life of suffering, pretending, and striving to reach a level of peace, joy, and thriving?

No.

How do we go from Nothing is Magical to Everything is Magical?

Is there a passport? Do you need to share your blood type? Is it bus number 17?

Let's pull into the station.

1. I meditate.
2. I create.

If I do one without the other, I'm either floating too much or too grounded. I need both to rocket forward, to live on my just-above-the-ground plane of a frequency where I'm pulled and not pushing, I'm thriving and not surviving, I'm me of today and not me of the past.

In other books, I talk about the cat. The one with 9 lives. Then I mention that I'm not a cat. I have this one life.

I don't want to apologize for living above ground. I want to rise up even further and reach and rise and relish.

Ooh, that just came out of me--and I love alliteration.

Reach, rise, relish.

Plus, relish is nice on a burger.
How can I go from floating in the heavens to a burger?
Because this is all light, easy, and simple.
It's fun and funny.
Because I'm both deliciously satisfied and I'm kinda hungry.
Because while there are days when I feel that <u>Nothing is Magical</u>, I can return to my default state where <u>Everything is Magical</u>.

1. Meditate (let it in).
2. Create (let it out).

I can add more steps and make it harder if you like. I can create a course and write books (oh wait, I did). I can charge you $497. You can fill out forms.

You can dream and hope. You can procrastinate and weigh the options. Wait until a future life--especially if you're a cat.

Or you can read into those two steps and live by them. It's all you need.

- **Possible:** you have no idea what I'm going on about in this chapter
- **Impossible:** nothing is magical
- **Repossible:** everything is magical

## MEDITATE + CREATE
THE (NO LONGER) SECRET FORMULA TO CREATIVE SUCCESS

"Meditation is to get insight, to get understanding and compassion, and when you have them, you are compelled to act."

— Thich Nhat Hanh

I've been a little stuck in the past few weeks. OK, months. How can I break free?

I'm busy! I'm getting things done. That's even an acronym, right? GTD. Check!

But where am I headed? What's my "Secret" project? And by secret, I mean, my passion project, the one I work on when I wake up early on a Sunday and everyone else is sleeping?

It took me an hour, but I got my answer.

- It came to me (**pull**) but then I also had to do some work to get it out (**push**).
- It came to me (**meditate**) but then I also had to do some work to get it out (**create**).

Here are a few minutes of clarity on a sunny Sunday morning in the woods, i.e. my office: create-meditate.repossible.com.

- **Possible:** meditate + create
- **Impossible:** meditate - create
- **Repossible:** meditate X create

# PART VIII

# THANK YOU

"Develop an attitude of gratitude, and give thanks for everything that happens to you, knowing that every step forward is a step toward achieving something bigger and better than your current situation."

— Brian Tracy

## 36

# A DIALOGUE WITHOUT AN AUDIENCE IS A MONOLOGUE
### THANK YOU FCR BEING HERE

> "We all need people who will give us feedback. That's how we improve."
>
> — BILL GATES

*I* could write, "I couldn't do this without you."
But of course I could. I write. I create. I get stuff done. I can do it with you or I could do it without you.

I put it out there, I publish books, I upload grainy videos of me recording unscripted performances in hopes I can get an idea across.

But it's going to be a whole lot more:

- Fun
- Rewarding
- Helpful
- Funny
- Better (yeah, "More better." That's good.)
- Edited
- Thought through

if we do this together.

"The shortest feedback loop I can think of is doing improvisation in front of an audience."

— Demetri Martin

Sure, I write books. You have one of them in your hands right now. In essence, it's a monologue. I write stuff and you read it.

That's fine and all.

But the dialogue is when things get good.

There are have been a gazillion links to videos of me (and others) in this book. Yet, how can we make this more of a two-way street? More of a dialogue than a monologue?

Over where the videos are hosted, you can leave comments. You could join the Repossible Facebook Group and say hi in there.

If you'd rather not get all that direct, you can also like the Repossible Facebook Page or comment there or follow or whatever it is we do with Facebook pages—I'm not even sure.

The #1 action you can take to help spread the Create love would be to write a quick and honest review of this book. I'll get into that in the next chapter called Ask.

But because we're still in the book, my challenge to you is to also start the dialogue with what you create. Sure, you can create in a vacuum, too (I do it all the time). But when you let the air in, when you open up the doors to the world and let your creations come into their own, that's where the magic happens.

So before we completely get into back of the book matter, I want you to know I wholeheartedly appreciate and cherish you being here and I thank you for your time, attention, and creations.

- **Possible:** monologue
- **Impossible:** Yule log
- **Repossible:** dialogue

# THANK YOU, MOM
## HERE WE GO

"If you like 'em if you love 'em tell 'em now."

— Mom (from a cowboy poem)

*I* have just added this little chapter at the end of the book as a tribute to my mom.

She passed away almost two months ago now and whereas the first 6 weeks after her passing were filled with administration and paperwork and filing, it has now been enough time to where I'm somewhat back in a routine.

But that routine is different.

That routine no longer includes calling her from the woods with Pepper in the evening. She was a large part of my daily inspiration.

The routine has changed.

I *want* that routine to change again, change more, change for the better, higher, greater.

I honor my mom's gift to the world and feel chosen, yes, by her, to fill her shoes and spread her positive attitude and endless energy to those around me.

Yesterday morning, during my meditation, she suggested I use my voice.

I took it to mean narrating audiobooks, recording podcasts, and making films.

The first thing I did yesterday morning was set up production on the Create audiobook and then I started cranking through the chapters.

As I recorded, I physically felt my body lightening. Letting off steam, opening the valve, unblocking the exhaust pipe.

For me, audio recording is one of my outlets.

What is one of yours?

Figure that out. Ask your mom. Then turn the handle and let it flow out of you.

The secret part that defies physics is that the more I let out, the more I narrate a book, the more that comes in. It seems like this would cost me energy yet it provides it.

Maybe that's what kept my mom going, pulled her forward and helped her lift up so many around her.

The "outpouring" of her love, her inspiration, and her energy was more of a river than a waterfall.

Although the source is mostly from within, allow those who fill your well to do so and your energy will be consistent, unstoppable, and effortless.

Oh, it's also fun. It's got to be fun.

To get an idea of the positive attitude my mom left for me—and left for all of us—check out create-mom.repossible.com.

- **Possible:** keep on keeping on
- **Impossible:** thank them after it's too late
- **Repossible:** honor those who went before you and rise up

# ASK
## THIS PART SCARES ME

"Learning to ask is like flexing a muscle. The more you do it, the easier it becomes. I started by learning how to ask for the small things in my life, and eventually I could make the Big Daunting Asks."

— Caroline Ghosn

What you have in your hands—or maybe in your ears—is my 23rd book. It's my baby, it's my passion, it's what I love to do.

I can write (monologue) and even record audio and video (a bit more interaction) but when it comes to the point where I actually, directly ask you to do something (dialogue), that's when things get awkward for me.

You just finished this book. I'm going to keep this short because you're done and you're ready to put this down and maybe go off into a dreamy sleep or head out on a run or ... I don't know what you're about to do. (What are you about to do? Just curious... ;-))

**So here's my last quick request: could you leave an honest review for this book?**

As an author, book reviews are incredibly important. They truly can make or break a book's success.

If you're not sure what to write, remember the chapter on "How did it make you feel?" I ask you now:

> *"How do you feel right now?"*
>
> *"Is there a tidbit from this book you can recall that someone you know might benefit from?"*
>
> *"Is there an action you're going to take?"*

Remember the Chinese proverb about when to plant a tree and how the best time was 20 years ago and the second best time was today? It doesn't apply to book reviews. The best time is today.

If, by chance, you think something was missing in the book or it just didn't "do it for you" and you'd like to share that, how about you send that note to me instead? ;-) Maybe I can then adapt the book towards that end? You can write me directly at create@likomaisland.com.

Thank you so very much for reading Create and especially for reading all the way to this point way back here. You're clearly one of those people who follow through, make progress, and get to the finish line.

- **Possible:** think about leaving a review
- **Impossible:** remember to do it next Thursday
- **Repossible:** leave a review right now

# ABOUT THE AUTHOR
## AND HIS INFATUATION WITH MORGAN FREEMAN

Bradley Charbonneau isn't going to write in the third person here. It's just weird.

I used to do it because I thought that's what you're supposed to do. Maybe you are.

But this is my 23rd book and I think I've earned the right to put the "About the Author" section in first person.

I mean, come on, it's not like I'm being interviewed here by Morgan Freeman.

On that note, and hey, here we are in the "About the Author" section so I can tell you completely dorky stuff about myself, I have a refrigerator magnet that says:

"I wish my life were narrated by Morgan Freeman."

— The Fridge

Oddly, it **sums up my whole life** and why **I write books** in that one little magnet. I can hear you thinking right this second:

"Gee, that's a little bizarre, Bradley. How so?"

— You (in your head)

When Morgan Freeman reads something or even just speaks and talks about, oh, I don't know, vegetables, it's as if it's more important than anything else going on at that time, you're somehow engaged, entranced even, and hanging on his every word as if he's some 108-year-old guru from Nepal who only speaks on the lunar eclipse and then is quiet again.

This is **exactly** what I'm getting at with my message:

Our lives, our paths, our day-to-day events and actions are what they are and, yes, we can influence them and alter the path we're on.

But whatever direction we take, whatever action we begin today, whatever we create, it's going to sound better, it's going to actually be better, when we see ourselves as **special**, **unique**, and **magical**.

Remember back to "The Secret of Kite Hill" (my first book I wrote together with my two sons when they were 8 and 10). At its core, it's a book about a walk home from school.

Simple, even mundane.

Yet it's transformed into a deeper story, an example of how a tiny, *seemingly insignificant* event has mutated into something much bigger.

Think about it. If Morgan Freeman were to narrate "The Secret of Kite Hill," it would elevate the story to epic proportions, to history-making drama, and turn something ordinary into something extraordinary.

This is exactly, precisely, and purely what I'm after.

**The ordinary into the extraordinary.**

Maybe I can get this guy to read my "About the Author" page if Morgan Freeman is busy: https://youtu.be/ofEhGzguBYI

Until then, I'll keep living Every Single Day as if my life is narrated by Morgan Freeman—and if he's busy and the other guy, too, then I know another narrator who could tell your story better than anyone else on the planet.

That person is, of course, you.

I live in a little town in the woods outside of Utrecht in The Netherlands with my wife Saskia, our famous two young boys of "The Adventures of Li & Lu" fame, and our at-least-as-famous dog Pepper.

This is my twenty-third book.

It is far, far, far from my last.

*Find, ask, decide, create, and play at:*
bradleycharbonneau.com

- **Possible:** silence
- **Impossible:** Morgan Freeman
- **Repossible:** your own voice

    facebook.com/bradley.charbonneau.author
    twitter.com/brathocha
    instagram.com/brathocha
    pinterest.com/likoma
    bookbub.com/profile/bradley-charbonneau

# ACKNOWLEDGMENTS
## BETTER TOGETHER

Ever since I wrote Spark (and interviewed 13 families for it), I value more and more ~~working~~ playing together with others. Do we have time for one last numbered list?

**Here's what happens when you play together with others:**

1. Fun
2. Better
3. Unknown creative ideas come your way
4. Together
5. Better Together
6. New ideas
7. Ideas that are not yours—nor would you have ever thought of them on your own.
8. Laughter
9. Cold, hard, truth (do you like how this one follows laughter?)
10. Grit
11. Accountability
12. Funny

13. Cooperation
14. Collaboration
15. New projects
16. Reigning in from too many "New projects"
17. Balance

**Nicoline Huizinga** just wrote a note in my shared Google Doc listing her favorite subtitles and I think we have a winner! **Daniel Oppenheim** texted with me back and forth early on a Sunday morning all the way from Slovenia with some wild ideas about subtitles (that may or may not make the final cut but they *guide the discussion* and *broaden the scope*).

**Sudhanya Mallick** helped with a long overdue photoshoot and that seemingly insignificant afternoon has turned into a partnership part of which is the creation of the Create Summit.

**Adwynna MacKenzie** and **Dede Charbonneau** (yes, that Dede, my mom!) dare to delve into the depths of a poorly formatted Google Doc manuscript and take out words I overuse such as "just" and "that." They also dare ask me the hard questions like, "What in the world are you talking about in Chapter X?"

**Ivo d'Haens** tackled subtitles, design, and anything else I lobbed over the wall—and he tossed it back with markups and red pens and it became better with each round.

I'd like to thank my new designer, **Anne Mitchelson**, for surrendering to my desire of incorporating "vintage travel poster" style into the covers. Then, the best part of working together, she steered me away from what I thought was the best idea to what she thought our audience and market thought was the best idea: a lighter, funnier, and yet at the same time more professional and branded cover design for the entirety of the Repossible series.

Yep, I could do all of this alone but it's more fun and just way more better to play together.

I thank you deeply and with a smile.

- **Possible:** you still think you have all of the best ideas
- **Impossible:** you actually do have all of the best ideas
- **Repossible:** oh so way better together

## ALSO BY BRADLEY CHARBONNEAU

Most of my books are also available as audiobooks (which I giddily narrate). Search for my name at your favorite audiobook distributor, slip on your headphones, and let me take you away.

### Repossible

Repossible

Every Single Day (+ Playbook)

Ask

Dare

Create

Decide

Meditate

Spark

Surrender

Play

Celebrate

Evaluate (2021)

Elevate (2021)

### Frequency

Every Single Day

Every Single Day Playbook

Every Single Day Kids

Every Single Day Teens (I want to write this one because I want to read this one...)

Every Single Day Parents

## Charlie Holiday

Now Is Your Chance (1)

Second Chance (2)

Chance of a Lifetime (3)

## For Creatives

Audio for Authors

Meditation for Creatives (2021)

## Shorts

Secret Bus to Paradise

Where I (Already) Am

Pass the Sour Cream

A Trip to Hel

Drive-By Dropping

## Li & Lu

The Secret of Kite Hill (1)

The Secret of Markree Castle (2)

The Key to Markree Castle (3)

The Gift of Markree Castle (4)

Driehoek (5)

# Really Old ...

urban travel guide SAN FRANCISCO

**THE END**

*I*t's really the beginning.
 Go ahead: create.

# AFTERWORD

We Asked, we Dared to answer the question, and Created daily habits towards our great future.

What's next?

- Decide
- Meditate
- Spark

Thanks for reading. I hope these words bring through to you the power I feel when they leave my fingers.

Bradley Charbonneau

www.ingramcontent.com/pod-product-compliance
Lightning Source LLC
LaVergne TN
LVHW051111080426
835510LV00018B/1992